'*Uncanny Valley* is a different sort of Silicon Valley narrative, a literary-minded outsider's insider account of an insulated world that isn't as insular or distinctive as it and we assume ... Through Wiener's story, we begin to perceive how much tech owes its power, and the problems that come with it, to contented ignorance'   *Atlantic*

'Wiener has the two talents that every memoir needs: a devastating eye for detail ... and the ability to map her experience onto a cultural shift much larger than herself ... I deadened my phone and laptop while reading this so I could give it my Undivided Attention. I'm recommending not only the book but also this reading method'   *Vulture*

'Studded with sharp assessments'   *Washington Post*

'Hyper-self-aware ... Throughout the memoir, Wiener sustains a piercing tone of crisp, arch observation'
San Francisco Chronicle

'Beautifully observed'   *Slate*

'An achingly relatable and sharply focused firsthand account ... the literary texture of Wiener's narrative makes it particularly valuable as a primary document of this moment. Her voice, alternating between cool and detached and impassioned and earnest, boasts an observational precision that is devastating. It is whip smart and searingly funny'   *Nation*

'A hyper-detailed, thoroughly engrossing memoir ... At the intersection of exploitative labor, entitled men, and ungodly amounts of money, Wiener bears witness to the fearsome future as it unfolds'
Esquire

'I raced through it ... Wiener's colleagues are so fanatical about emojis that she becomes "embarrassed by the thought of using my laptop in public spaces – my work looked like a video game for children". And these people control the fountainhead of modern power and culture! San Francisco is a city of spoilt evil children who think they know best. Read this book and be afraid'
The Times

'Incisive ... inherently timely. Its style is of a part with the dry, affectless writing of the period that Wiener seeks to capture but goes beyond the Sally Rooney-Tao Lin axis to deliver something sharper and more complete ... I tore through *Uncanny Valley*, riveted by the wit and precision of Wiener's observations'
Baffler

'Illuminating ... Wiener's empathy makes the portrait all the more damning'
Chicago Tribune

'Wiener shines when she turns her incisive observations on the many entitled men running amok in Silicon Valley ... an engaging summary of every terrible thing you've heard about start-ups'
A.V. Club

'Eschewing the caffeinated, self-referential keenness that defined the decade's online writing, Wiener is cerebral and diagnostic in her observance of escalating corporate surveillance'
Paris Review

'A rare mix of acute, funny, up-to-the-minute social observation, dead-serious contemplation of the tech industry's annexation of our lives, and a sincere first-person search for meaningful work and connection. How does an unworn pair of plain sneakers "become a monument to the end of sensuousness"? Read on'

WILLIAM FINNEGAN, author of *Barbarian Days: A Surfing Life*

'An addictive combination of coming-of-age story, journalistic memoir, and brilliant social critique. This is a stunningly good book. I loved it' DANI SHAPIRO, author of *Inheritance*

'A sentimental education for our accelerated times, a memoir so good it will make you slow down. Is it too much to say that every sculpted page will be studied by future generations? (No.) Anna Wiener is the Joan Didion of start-up culture and then some' ED PARK, author of *Personal Days*

'Equal parts enchanting and subversive … [Wiener's] account of living inside the Bay Area bubble reads like HBO's Silicon Valley filtered through Renata Adler; Wiener is a trenchant cultural cartographer, mapping out a foggy world whose ruling class is fueled by empty scripts: "People were saying nothing, and saying it all the time". The book's author does the very opposite' *Vogue*

UNCANNY VALLEY

SEDUCTION AND DISILLUSIONMENT IN SAN FRANCISCO'S STARTUP SCENE

ANNA WIENER

4th ESTATE • London

4th Estate
An imprint of HarperCollins*Publishers*
1 London Bridge Street
London SE1 9GF

www.4thEstate.co.uk

First published in Great Britain in 2020 by 4th Estate
First published in the United States by MCD in 2020
This 4th Estate paperback edition published in 2021

1

A catalogue record for this book is
available from the British Library

ISBN 978-0-0-0829686-5

This book is a memoir. It reflects the author's present recollections
of experiences over time. In some instances, events have
been compressed and dialogue has been re-created.
The names and identifying characteristics of some persons
described in the book have been changed.

Printed and bound in Great Britain by
CPI Group (UK) Ltd, Croydon

MIX
Paper from
responsible sources
FSC™ C007454

This book is produced from independently certified FSC™ paper
to ensure responsible forest management.

For more information visit: www.harpercollins.co.uk/green

INCENTIVES

Depending on whom you ask, it was either the apex, the inflection point, or the beginning of the end for Silicon Valley's startup scene—what cynics called a bubble, optimists called the future, and my future coworkers, high on the fumes of world-historical potential, breathlessly called the ecosystem. A social network everyone said they hated but no one could stop logging in to went public at a valuation of one-hundred-odd billion dollars, its grinning founder ringing the opening bell over video chat, a death knell for affordable rent in San Francisco. Two hundred million people signed on to a microblogging platform that helped them feel close to celebrities and other strangers they'd loathe in real life. Artificial intelligence and virtual reality were coming into vogue, again. Self-driving cars were considered inevitable. Everything was moving to mobile. Everything was up in the cloud. The cloud was an unmarked data center in the middle of Texas or Cork or Bavaria, but nobody cared. Everyone trusted it anyway.

It was a year of new optimism: the optimism of no hurdles, no limits, no bad ideas. The optimism of capital, power, and opportunity. Wherever money changed hands, enterprising technologists and MBAs were bound to follow. The word "disruption" proliferated, and everything was ripe for or vulnerable to it: sheet music, tuxedo rentals, home cooking, home buying, wedding planning, banking, shaving, credit lines, dry cleaning, the rhythm method. A website that allowed people to rent out their unused driveways raised four million dollars from elite firms on Sand Hill Road. A website taking on the kennel market—a pet-sitting and dog-walking app that disrupted neighborhood twelve-year-olds—raised ten million. An app for coupon-clipping enabled an untold number of bored and curious urbanites to pay for services they never knew they needed, and for a while people were mainlining antiwrinkle toxins, taking trapeze lessons, and bleaching their assholes, just because they could do it at a discount.

It was the dawn of the era of the unicorns: startups valued, by their investors, at over a billion dollars. A prominent venture capitalist had declared in the op-ed pages of an international business newspaper that software was eating the world, a claim that was subsequently cited in countless pitch decks and press releases and job listings as if it were proof of something—as if it were not just a clumsy and unpoetic metaphor, but evidence.

Outside of Silicon Valley, there seemed to be an overall resistance to taking any of it too seriously. There was a prevailing sentiment that, just like the last bubble, this would eventually pass. Meanwhile, the industry expanded beyond the province of futurists and hardware enthusiasts, and settled into its new role as the scaffolding of everyday life.

Not that I was aware of any of this—not that I was paying any attention at all. I didn't even have apps on my phone. I had just turned twenty-five and was living on the edge of Brooklyn with a roommate I hardly knew, in an apartment filled with so much secondhand furniture it almost had a connection to history. I had a fragile but agreeable life: a job as an assistant at a small literary agency in Manhattan; a smattering of beloved friends on whom I exercised my social anxiety, primarily by avoiding them.

But the corners seemed to be coming up. The wheels were coming off. I thought, every day, about applying to graduate school. My job was running its course. There was no room to grow, and after three years the voyeuristic thrill of answering someone else's phone had worn thin. I no longer wanted to amuse myself with submissions from the slush pile, or continue filing author contracts and royalty statements in places where they did not belong, like my desk drawer. My freelance work, proofreading and copyediting manuscripts for a small press, was also waning in volume, because I had recently broken up with the editor who assigned it to me. The relationship had been stressful, but reliably consuming: the editor, several years my senior, had talked about marriage but wouldn't stop cheating. These infidelities were revealed after he borrowed my laptop for a weekend and returned it without logging out of his accounts, where I read a series of romantic and brooding private messages he exchanged with a voluptuous folk singer via the social network everyone hated. That year, I hated it extra.

I was oblivious to Silicon Valley, and contentedly so. It's not that I was a Luddite—I could point-and-click before I could read. I just never opened the business section. Like anyone else with a desk job, I spent the majority of my waking hours peering into a computer, typing and tabbing through the days, the web browser a current of digital digression running beneath my work. At home, I wasted time scrolling through the photos and errant musings of people I should have long since forgotten, and exchanged endless, searching emails with friends, in which we swapped inexpert professional and dating advice. I read the online archives of literary magazines that no longer existed, digitally window-shopped for clothing I could not afford, and created and abandoned private, aspirational blogs with names like *A Meaningful Life*, in the vain hope that they might push me closer to leading one. Still, it never occurred to me that I might someday become one of the people working behind the internet, because I had never considered that there were people behind the internet at all.

In the manner of so many twentysomethings living in North Brooklyn at a time when an artisanal chocolate factory was considered a local landmark and people spoke earnestly about urban homesteading, my life was affectedly analog. I took photographs with an old, medium-format camera that had belonged to my grandfather, then scanned those photographs into my dying laptop, its internal fan whirring, to upload to my blogs. I sat atop busted amplifiers and cold radiators in Bushwick practice spaces, paging through back issues of prestige magazines, watching various crushes suck on hand-rolled cigarettes and finger their drumsticks and slide guitars, listening attentively to their noodling in preparation for my feedback to be solicited, though it never was. I went on dates with men who made chapbooks or live-edge wood furniture; one identified as an experimental baker. My to-do list always included archaic chores like buying a new needle for the record player I rarely used or a battery for the watch I never remembered to wear. I refused to own a microwave.

Insofar as I considered the technology industry of any importance to my own life, it was only because of circulating concerns specific to my professional world. An online superstore that had gotten its start in the nineties by selling books on the World Wide Web—not because the founder had a love of literature, but because he had a love of consumers, and consumptive efficiency—had expanded to become a digital bargain basement dealing in appliances, electronics, groceries, mass fashion, children's toys, cutlery, and various nonnecessities manufactured in China. Having conquered the rest of retail, the online superstore had returned to its roots and seemed to be experimenting with various ways to destroy the publishing industry. It had even gone so far as to start its own publishing imprints, which my literary friends scorned and derided as cheesy and shameless. We ignored the fact that we had many reasons to be grateful to the website, as the publishing industry was being kept afloat by bestselling novels about sadomasochism and vampires who fucked, hatched in the incubator of the online superstore's marketplace for self-published e-books. Within a few years, the founder, a chelonian ex–hedge funder, would become the wealthiest person in the world and undergo a montage-worthy makeover, but at the time we weren't thinking about him. All that mattered to us was that the site was responsible for half of all book sales, which meant it had wrested control of the most important levers: pricing and distribution. It had us in its grip.

I did not know that the tech industry fetishized the online superstore for its cutthroat, data-driven company culture, or that its proprietary recommendation algorithms, which suggested vacuum cleaner bags and diapers alongside novels about dysfunctional families, were considered cutting-edge, admirable, and at the fore of applied machine learning. I did not know that the online superstore also had a lucrative sister business selling cloud-computing services—metered use of a sprawling, international network of server farms—which provided the back-end infrastructure for other companies' websites and apps. I did not know that it was nearly impossible to use the internet at all without enriching the online superstore or its founder. I only knew that I was expected to loathe both, and I did—loudly, at any opportunity, and with righteous indignation.

On the whole, the tech industry was a distant and abstract concern. That fall, publishing was reeling from the proposed merger of the two largest houses, which together employed some ten thousand people and whose combined value pushed past two billion dollars. A two-billion-dollar company: the power and money were unfathomable to me. If anything could protect us from the online superstore, I thought, it was a two-billion-dollar company. I did not know about the twelve-employee unicorns.

Later, once I had settled into my life in San Francisco, I would learn that the year I spent drinking in dive bars with friends from the publishing industry, moaning about our impossible futures, was the same year many of my new friends, coworkers, and crushes swiftly and quietly made their first millions. While some of these friends were starting companies or embarking on two-year, self-imposed sabbaticals in their mid-twenties, I was sitting at a narrow desk outside of my boss's office, tracking the agency's expenses and trying to determine my value using my annual salary—increased, the previous winter, from twenty-nine thousand dollars to thirty—as a unit of measurement. What was my value? Five times as much as our new office sofa; twenty orders of customized stationery. While my future peers were hiring wealth advisers and going on meditation retreats in Bali to pursue self-actualization, I was vacuuming roaches off the walls of my rental apartment, smoking weed, and bicycling to warehouse concerts along the East River, staving off a thrumming sense of dread.

It was a year of promise, excess, optimism, acceleration, and hope—in some other city, in some other industry, in someone else's life.

Lightly hungover one afternoon, eating a limp salad at the literary agency, I read an article about a startup that had raised three million dollars to bring a revolution to book publishing. The story led with a photo of the three cofounders, men who smiled widely against a pastoral background, like fraternity brothers posing for a graduation shot. All three wore button-down shirts; they looked like they had just shared a good chuckle. They looked so at ease, so convincing. They looked like the sort of men who used electric toothbrushes and never shopped at thrift stores, who followed the stock market and kept their dirty napkins off the table. The sort of men around whom I always felt invisible.

According to the news item, the revolution would come via an e-reading app for mobile phones that operated on a subscription model. This sounded niche to me, and the app's pitch—access to a sprawling library of e-books for a modest monthly fee—seemed like the sort of promise that came with a lot of fine print. Still, something about the idea appealed.

The e-reading app was a new concept for publishing, where new ideas rarely emerged and were never rewarded. It didn't help that publishing felt always on the brink of collapse. It was not just the monopolistic online superstore, or the two-billion-dollar merger, though these compounded and accelerated our anxieties. It was also the mores. The only way to have a successful and sustainable career in the publishing industry, it seemed, was to inherit money, marry rich, or wait for peers to defect or die.

Among the assistant class, my friends and I wondered whether there would be a place for us as the industry continued to shrink. A person could live on thirty thousand dollars a year in New York; millions did more with less. But take-home pay of seventeen hundred dollars a month was difficult to square with the social, festive, affluent lifestyle the publishing industry encouraged: networking drinks, dinner parties, three-hundred-dollar wrap dresses, built-in bookcases in Fort Greene or Brooklyn Heights. It was nice to get new hardcover books for free, but it would be nicer if we could afford to buy them.

Every assistant I knew quietly relied on a secondary source of income: copyediting, bartending, waitressing, generous relatives. These cash flows were rarely disclosed to anyone but each other. It was an indignity to talk about money when our superiors, who ordered poached salmon and glasses of rosé at lunch, seemed to consider low pay a rite of passage, rather than systemic exploitation in which they might feel some solidarity. Solidarity, specifically, with us.

The truth was that we were expendable. There were more English majors with independent financial support and strings of unpaid literary internships than there were open positions at agencies and houses. The talent pool was self-replenishing. Men in beige desert boots and women in mustard-yellow cardigans waited in the wings, clutching their cream-colored résumés. The industry relied, to some degree, on a high rate of attrition.

Still, my publishing friends and I were stubborn. We liked working with books; we clung to our cultural capital. There was a pervasive resentment around paying our dues, but we were prepared to pay them. A selective moral logic seemed to animate the industry: publishing had failed to innovate quickly, yes, but surely we—the literary, the passionate, lovers and defenders of human expression—wouldn't lose to companies whose executives didn't even show an appreciation for books. We had taste and integrity. We were nervous, and very broke.

I was very broke. Not poor, never poor. Privileged and downwardly mobile. Like many of my peers, I could afford to work in publishing because I had a safety net. I had graduated college debt-free, by no accomplishment of my own: my parents and grandparents had saved for my tuition since I was a blur on the sonogram. I had no dependents. I had secret, minor credit-card debt, but I did not want to ask for help. Borrowing money to make rent, or pay off a medical bill, or even, in a fit of misguided aspiration, buy my own wrap dress, always felt like a multifront failure. I was ashamed that I couldn't support myself, and ashamed that my generous, forgiving parents were effectively subsidizing a successful literary agency. I had one year left on their health insurance. The situation was not sustainable. I was not sustainable.

My parents had always hoped that I would professionalize in medicine or law, immerse myself in something stable and safe. They were comfortable—my mother was a writer, and worked with nonprofits, and my father was in financial services—but they emphasized independence. My brother, who had graduated pre-recession, already had a successful career by the time he was my age. None of them understood the slow burn of the publishing hierarchy or the industry's shabby, nostalgic glamour. My mother often asked, gently, why I was still an assistant— making coffee, taking coats—at twenty-five. She wasn't asking for a structural explanation.

My desires were generic. I wanted to find my place in the world, and be independent, useful, and good. I wanted to make money, because I wanted to feel affirmed, confident, and valued. I wanted to be taken seriously. Mostly, I didn't want anyone to worry about me.

Though I had the nagging suspicion that the e-book startup's cofounders might be jockeying for a place on the wrong side of the issues I cared about—the side of the online superstore, the side that was already winning—at the expense of publishers, authors, and agents, I envied their sense of entitlement to the future. There was something unusual and attractive about people who had a vision for how the industry could evolve and a green light to get it done.

I didn't know that three million dollars was considered a modest fund-raising round. I didn't know that most startups raised money more than once, and three million dollars was experimental, pocket change. To me, that amount of money was a flag in the ground, an indication of permanence, as good as a blank check to go forth and take over. The future of publishing was here, I assumed. I wanted in.

I joined the e-book startup at the beginning of 2013, after a series of ambiguous and casual interviews. I had been primed to have expectations of a certain techie stereotype—antisocial and unwashed, sex starved and awkward—but the cofounders, who would never have referred to themselves as techies, immediately confounded this. The CEO was fast-moving, confident, and chiseled, and the chief technical officer, a soft-spoken systems thinker, was humble and patient. The creative founder, who referred to himself as the chief product officer, was an easy favorite. He had gone to art school on the East Coast and wore jeans that were so tight I felt I already knew him: he was like my friends from college, but successful. I was older than all three of them.

Conversation with the cofounders had been so easy, and the interviews so much more like coffee dates than the formal, sweaty-blazer interrogations I had experienced elsewhere, that at a certain point I wondered if maybe the three of them just wanted to hang out. They had, after all, recently moved across the country. It wasn't like they wanted to live in New York—it was clear that they would have preferred the energy out west—but they needed to be closer to the industry they were disrupting, to build partnerships. Like the patron saint of mislaid sympathies, I speculated that perhaps they were just lonely.

They were, of course, not lonely. They were focused and content. All three were clean-shaven and had good skin. They wore shirts that were always crisp and modestly buttoned to the clavicle. They were in long-term relationships with high-functioning women, women with great hair with whom they exercised and shared meals at restaurants that required reservations. They lived in one-bedroom apartments in downtown Manhattan and had no apparent need for psychotherapy. They shared a vision and a game plan. They weren't ashamed to talk about it, weren't ashamed to be openly ambitious. Fresh off impressive positions and prestigious summer internships at large tech corporations in the Bay Area, they spoke about their work like industry veterans, lifelong company men. They were generous with their unsolicited business advice, as though they hadn't just worked someplace for a year or two but built storied careers. They were aspirational. I wanted, so much, to be like— and liked by—them.

Because the role had been created specifically for me, the job was a three-month trial run. The scope and responsibilities were nebulous to all of us: some curating of in-app titles, some copywriting, various secretarial tasks. As a full-time contractor, I would be paid twenty dollars an hour, again with no benefits. The money didn't look like much up front, but I calculated the annual salary and was gratified to see that it would amount to forty thousand dollars.

My friends in publishing were skeptical when I told them where I was going to work. They had a lot of questions I felt uneasy answering. Wouldn't a subscription model undercut author royalties? Wasn't it basically a cynical, capitalist appropriation of the public library system? Wasn't an app like this parasitic at best? Was it all that different from the online superstore, and wouldn't the app's success come at the expense of the literary culture and community? I didn't have a good response to most of these concerns. Mostly, I tried not to think about them. Smug and self-congratulatory, I translated most of my friends' questions to mean, simply, *What about us?*

The startup's office was a block from Canal Street, in a neighborhood the CEO called Nolita, the CTO called Little Italy, and the CPO called Chinatown. The surrounding area was tourist-addled even on weekdays, brimming with adults popping overstuffed cannoli and shooting tiny paper cups of espresso while their children eyeballed storefront displays of dusty parmesan wheels. The office was not so much an office as a spare table in the loftlike headquarters of a more established startup, one that enabled people to buy and sell art on the internet, at auction—a business model I did not fully understand, as the fun of auctions, I had always imagined, was the performative, feverish display of wealth and one-upmanship. I did not realize at the time that for people in the tech industry, such expressions of wealth were not just gauche but antiquated. There was nothing more civilized than hiding your money behind a browser.

The loft had creaky wood floors and a long kitchen counter running along one wall, which bore an assembly of pour-over vessels and sacks of small-batch coffee beans from local roasters. The bathrooms had showers. On my start date, I arrived at the table to find a welcome gift: a stack of hardcover books about technology, inscribed by the founders and stamped with a wax seal of the company logo: an oyster, unavoidably yonic, with a perfect pearl.

The e-book startup had millions in funding and job titles that suggested a robust and organized workforce, but the app itself was still in private alpha, used only by a handful of friends, family, and investors. There was only one other employee, a mobile engineer named Cam, whom the founders had been excited to hire away from a photo-editing app. The five of us sat around our mahogany table at the back of the loft, drinking coffee, as if in a perpetual board meeting.

For the first time in my career, I had some expertise. The men asked for my opinions—on the app's reading experience, on the quality of the inventory, on how best to ingratiate ourselves with online reading communities—and listened for the answers. Despite misunderstanding the technical infrastructure and having little insight into strategy, I felt useful. It was thrilling to watch the moving parts of a business come together; to feel that I could contribute.

•

To celebrate the CTO's birthday, we traveled to Midtown to see a movie about counterterrorism specialists. The movie opened with an audio montage of telephone calls made by people trapped in the World Trade Center on September 11. I did not want to continue watching, but more than that I did not know how to exit gracefully without having to explain that I had seen all of it happen at age fourteen, from the window of my high school Spanish classroom, four blocks away from the towers.

I considered faking something biological: gastroenteritis, menstruation. I considered the Irish goodbye. I resented that I had not done my research on the film, resented that I could not be a normal person with normal experiences doing a normal thing, like enjoying an action movie with my colleagues, without getting mired in unresolved PTSD. I fidgeted so badly that I lost an earring in the theater, and when the lights came up after the credits, the CTO got down on his knees to search for it, beckoning the others to join. I was embarrassed to see them scrambling across the floor, and moved that they would run their palms over the sticky synthetic carpet for me. After waiting for a few seconds, I exclaimed that I had found it, and the boys stood up to button their jackets and heave on their backpacks; nobody noticed when I removed the remaining earring and shoved it into the lint of my pocket.

We moved into the late winter light, and walked to a Japanese dessert bar around the corner. I had never been to a dessert bar, let alone a Japanese one. The boys were delighted by the variety. They reminded one another that this was on the company card, and overordered. Sitting with the four of them, watching as they dipped their spoons into each other's desserts, resisting as they pushed their plates toward me to make sure

I tasted everything, I tried to imagine what the other patrons thought about our group. I felt like a babysitter, a fifth wheel, a chaperone, a little sister, a ball and chain, a concubine. I felt indescribably lucky. At the end of the night, I walked downtown alone to the farthest possible subway station, savoring.

I befriended Cam, the other employee who was not a founder. During our lunch breaks we would venture forth into the neighborhood and return with sandwiches or leaky plastic containers of Vietnamese takeout, which we would eat in the conference room while he patiently answered my questions about the difference between front-end development and back-end programming. On occasion, we would talk about the burdens and responsibilities of being employees one and two of a startup that, despite not yet having a public product, was already considered hot. "I think this is a really good time for us to join the company," he would reassure me. "I think we're very well positioned." He either did not know that I was a contractor, or was optimistic that I would be hired as a proper employee after the trial period.

Cam had a gentle, low-key nature. He loved his girlfriend, and her cat, and I loved hearing him talk about them. The only time I ever saw him get worked up was when I organized a company book club and none of the cofounders followed through. They were too busy building the app, they said. Who had time for book clubs? I understood this and did not particularly mind, but Cam chastened them in the company chat room and then took me out for soup. He insisted that they were rude and in the wrong; he insisted that I was working incredibly hard to build the company culture.

This was only partially true. After the first few weeks, during which I wrote website copy, tried to help recruit engineers from a short list of top universities, and edited the user privacy agreement to make it sound more like a friend than a lawyer, it seemed that mostly the founders were overpaying me to look for a more permanent office space and order them snacks: single-serving bags of cheese crackers, tiny chocolate bars, cups of blueberry yogurt.

The concept of eating a snack at work was new to me. At the literary agency, eating at work during non-lunch hours was a source of not-insignificant shame, and gnawing at a bagel or crunching through a bag of bodega pretzels was, I thought, regarded as sloppy and unprofessional. In previous jobs, my inability to keep my homemade lunch untouched until lunchtime was an expression of my lack of self-control, the reason I still had baby fat at an age when the fat might have been postpartum, but instead was just me; I was the baby. The boys, by contrast, snacked throughout the day. They ate chips at their computers and dusted their hands off on paper towels, swished seltzer water and crumpled the cans beside their keyboards. I meticulously noted their preferences and tried to keep things interesting: a box of clementines one week, bags of cheddar popcorn the next.

With Cam in mind, I took it upon myself to bolster the company culture. I persisted with the book club, and the founders continued to snub it. I organized team outings, including one to a gilded private library that had belonged to a famed financier, a goliath of nineteenth-century banking. We wandered the building, admiring the imposing floor-to-ceiling bookcases, the twisting staircases and gold-painted ceiling, taking photographs and posting them to social media. This was how the app should feel, we all agreed: luxurious, but not intimidating; infinite.

The private library was a hit, but the truth was that three men in their early twenties with millions in the bank did not need me to take them on reading-themed field trips. It would be

more cost-effective for them to order their own snacks. Despite
Cam's encouragement, they also did not need me to build the
company culture. They did not really need me for anything. The
culture, insofar as our tiny company had one, revolved around
the founders. While they sometimes bickered, I never saw anyone leave the conference room angry. They seemed to be hap-
piest unwinding on the overstuffed couch, playing video games
together and drinking domestic beers. They did not need to
team-build or bond, and mostly that wasn't what we were doing.
We were building a company—or they were, and I was watching.

When we did find a new office space, on a prime block in the
west twenties—a part of the city some referred to, in an act of
taxonomic hubris, as Silicon Alley—it also belonged to another
startup, but this time the circumstances were different. The
lease-holding startup was working on something in the media
space, and its headcount had grown and shrunk as if the company were weight-cycling. At a team meeting, our CEO gravely
noted that the media startup had already pivoted multiple times
over. I asked what he meant by this, and all four men looked
at me suspiciously. Pivoting meant that they had changed their
business model in an effort to generate revenue. Pivoting meant
they were worried about runway. Pivoting meant they were a
cautionary tale. Only the two cofounders were left, tucked off
to the side. Everyone else had been let go once funding ran out.

The specter of these laid-off employees lingered, a reminder
to work harder. Most of our days were spent heads-down at
our desks, furiously instant-messaging each other from across
the underfurnished office. We took synchronized lunches and
talked about strategy. We returned to our computers and as-
siduously avoided eye contact. We held long and impassioned

meetings about partnerships and design, and ordered in pizza when these meetings crossed into night. Everything felt urgent, high stakes.

One afternoon, the CEO summoned us into a conference room to demo the pitch deck he was making for meetings with publishers. He opened by stating that ours was the era of the sharing economy. Millennials, he said, as if he were not one of them, weren't into ownership, but experiences. This was not just a new market strategy, but a cultural ideology. Pioneering digital platforms in the sharing and subscription economies enabled people to stream films and albums and video games, rent cocktail dresses and three-piece suits, reserve bedrooms in strangers' houses, and ride shotgun in strangers' cars. Music, movies, television, retail, and transportation had been disrupted. The time had come for books. The CEO flipped to a slide that displayed the logos of various successful subscription platforms, with our logo at the center.

Technology products were lifestyle products, the CEO said. As he continued his pitch, it became clear to me that the utility of the e-reading app was not so much about reading as it was about signaling that you were the type of person who *would* read, and who would use an app with a cutting-edge reading experience and innovative, intuitive design. The ideal user of the app, I deduced, was a person who thought of themselves as a reader, but wasn't, not really: licensing cost money, and anyone reading more than a few books a month could generate a licensing expense exceeding the subscription fee. Books were an opportunity, I understood, but not the endgame. It was just one type of content, and only the first step. Expansion: *that* was the endgame. Probably. I trusted them to figure it out.

The CEO did not acknowledge that the reason millennials

might be interested in experiences—like the experience of renting things they could never own—was related to student loan debt, or the recession, or the plummeting market value of cultural products in an age of digital distribution. There were no crises in this vision of the future. There were only opportunities.

I tried to determine whether I could believe in this. The CEO was charming, and committed to the company and its vision. Perhaps he and the other two founders were also brilliant. Their investors in Silicon Valley must have thought so. But they seemed to be least interested in the part of the business I cared about most—the books. "Hemingway" had been misspelled in the CEO's pitch deck: two *m*'s.

More relevantly, the model—starting with books, and taking it from there—seemed to hew all too closely to that of the online superstore. I began to wonder why it was, exactly, that they had hired me. I had been operating under the vain premise that it was because I knew something about books: I could be a bridge between the old and new guards. I had fancied myself a translator; I had fancied myself essential. Later, once I better understood the industry-wide interest in promoting women in tech—if not up the ranks, then at least in corporate marketing materials—I would allow myself to consider that perhaps I was more important to the aesthetic than critical to the business.

What I also did not understand at the time was that the founders had all hoped I would make my own job, without deliberate instruction. The mark of a hustler, a true entrepreneurial spirit, was creating the job that you wanted and making it look indispensable, even if it was institutionally unnecessary. This was an existential strategy for the tech industry itself, and it did not come naturally to me. My imagination was still tailored to the parameters of publishing: I suggested that the e-book startup host a reading series, as a form of outreach to the literary community. Perhaps we should have a book blog, I mused. Instead, the startup sent third-wave-coffee trucks to distribute free espresso drinks and pastries at industry conferences, where exciting swag historically meant a cotton tote bag or an advance reader's copy of a debut work of literary fiction. I had trouble strategizing at scale.

"She's too interested in learning, not doing," the CEO typed once into the company chat room. This was an accident—he meant it only for the other two cofounders. We huddled in the conference room and he apologized sincerely, while I looped the words over and over in my head. I had always been interested in learning, and I had always been rewarded for it; learning was what I did best. I wasn't used to having the sort of professional license and latitude that the founders were given. I lacked their confidence, their entitlement. I did not know about startup maxims to experiment and "own" things. I had never heard the common tech incantation *Ask forgiveness, not permission*.

In an effort to self-educate, I read blog posts about the startup mentality and did my best to imitate it. The CEO had published one a year earlier titled "How to Make an Impact During the First Month of Your Startup Job," and I resented myself for missing the writing on the wall. Take ownership, he had advised in the post. Be optimistic. Write down your opinions.

In the end, I resorted to writing long, embarrassing, and unsolicited emails to the founders, declaring my passion for reading. An e-reading app needed a passionate reader on staff, I was sure of it—maybe I didn't know how to be a good startup employee, at least not yet, but surely they would benefit from having me, a focus group of one, on the team anyway. After several long and heartfelt emails and another painful one-on-one huddle in the conference room, it was clear that there was no way I could stay. This was not the right moment in the company's journey, they said, for someone like me to get up to speed. The areas where I could add value would not be active for some time.

The cofounders all wanted to help me find a new job. They assumed I wanted to continue working in tech, and I didn't disabuse them of this. I was reluctant to return to publishing. I had tried to strike out on my own and had failed. Besides, I had been traitorous, joining a startup trying to rock the book world, and did not want to face the possibility that I might now be unwelcome.

I had also been spoiled by the speed and open-mindedness of the tech industry, the optimism and sense of possibility. In publishing, no one I knew was ever celebrating a promotion. Nobody my age was excited about what might come next. Tech, by comparison, promised what so few industries or institutions could, at the time: a future.

Most of the founders' professional network—the other startups in their venture capitalists' portfolios—lived in the Bay Area. The CPO spoke wistfully of California. "I maintain that San Francisco is the best place to be a young person," he told me. "You should really try to get out there before too long." I wanted to tell him that I thought I was still young: I was only twenty-five. Instead, I told him I would try.

Everyone I knew in San Francisco had already left. Our college class had graduated straight into a recession, and while most of us trudged to New York or Boston to compete for unpaid internships and other scraps of a ravaged economy, those who moved west refused to bend to despair. They chose instead to hide out for a while, work on their art. They lived in sun-flooded apartments, took part-time service jobs, and had complicated, consuming social lives. They freely experimented with hallucinogens and polyamory; smoked weed and slept in and day-drank; went to BDSM parties and wolfed burritos afterward. They started bands and did occasional sex work. They spent weekends in the mountains or the woods or on the beach, camping and hiking and participating in other wholesome activities that we made fun of back in New York.

This utopia was short-lived. It was being replaced by a late-capitalist hellscape, my friends reported. Rents were spiking. Art galleries and music venues were closing. Bars were overrun with men in their twenties wearing corporate-branded T-shirts, men who never finished their beers and complained whenever anyone on the sidewalk smoked a cigarette too close to the door. Men who wore stability running shoes to nightclubs. Men who said "K" instead of "thousand."

Dating websites were flooded with milquetoast strivers who earnestly listed business-management guides among their favorite books and arrived at dinner wearing backpacks stamped with the names of their employers. Young CEOs were showing up to sex parties expecting to play only with other young CEOs. My friends, covered in glitter and wearing tiny nut-hammocks and rolling on ecstasy, found themselves marching in the annual Pride parade alongside primary-colored, brand-consistent, family-friendly floats designed by heterosexual digital-marketing managers.

The city had begun to bend to the on-demand desires of recent college graduates with plump bank accounts. Even Oakland was becoming unaffordable for artists and writers working as loosely credentialed yoga instructors or grocery store cashiers. There weren't any jobs, my friends said, unless you wanted to work for a tech company. It went without saying that none of them did. Within a few years, they departed for gentrifying neighborhoods in New Orleans or Los Angeles, or found their way to graduate school, their flight paths and cross-country road trips doing double duty as funeral marches for a beloved city that, they all assured me, no longer existed.

When I traveled to San Francisco in the spring, to interview for a customer-support position at a data analytics startup, I didn't mention it to my ex–Bay Area friends. I dreaded how they would react if they knew I was angling for a job in the tech industry, that I had even a shred of interest in joining the people on whom they blamed their displacement—the people who had ruined their fun. I took the train from the airport into the city, feeling treacherous and estranged.

Using the millennial-friendly platform for renting strangers' bedrooms, I had booked a room in the Mission, in an apartment that belonged to a couple in their mid-fifties. It was my first time using the app, and as I stood on the front steps of an ornate Victorian, I felt like an orphan of nineteenth-century literature, a child on the brink of a new adventure. *Welcome home*, the home-sharing platform's marketing materials had gushed, exuding familial warmth with bright, bold colors. But while the website emphasized community, coziness, a richer life through new connections and novel experiences, my hosts greeted me coolly—a reminder that this was, above all, a transaction.

As the husband showed me around my room—guest towels in the hope chest, lemon tree in the backyard—he asked what had brought me to town. I explained with some trepidation that I was there to interview at a startup. I knew that the neighborhood had long been an enclave for artists, activists, and other groups without enough money to hold their own in housing court. I wanted to be sensitive. He nodded knowingly, without judgment, and shrugged. "We host full-time," he said. "I guess you could say we work for a startup, too."

Could I? He and his wife had both quit their day jobs, in the nonprofit sector, to provide the trappings of an authentic urban experience—different enough to be interesting, but generic enough to be comfortable—to tourists and interlopers like me. They slept in the basement. They weren't employees. They were part of the product.

It was my first time paying to stay with strangers. The apartment was clean and welcoming, full of overstuffed furniture and bowls of fruit, but I didn't know whether relaxing with a book on the sofa or borrowing kitchen implements to slice a ripe peach would be considered a breach of the home-sharing platform's terms of service—I'd only booked a room, after all. The policy had extensively covered the company's liability but didn't offer any specifics on how to behave. To play it safe, I walked carefully between my bedroom and the bathroom, as if the hallway were a grooved track—as if I were trespassing, intruding on a family and a life that did not belong to me.

The interview had been arranged with the help of the e-book startup's CEO, who advised that big data was a hot space. According to him, the analytics startup—just four years old, founded by college dropouts—had already infiltrated the market with impressive speed and ferocity. The company had twelve million dollars in venture funding, thousands of customers, and seventeen employees. "Our investors say they're the next unicorn," the e-book startup's CEO had enthused, tipping back in his chair. "It's a rocket ship." It was easy to get me to want something.

I was not particularly excited about customer support, but it was an entry-level job that required no programming knowledge. As a sociology major with a background in literary fiction and three months of experience in snack procurement, I assumed I was not in a position to be picky. The e-book startup's cofounders had been adamant that customer support was a temporary state. If I hustled, all three of them agreed, I would quickly find myself in a more interesting, autonomous, impressive role. I didn't know that in tech, qualifications—at least the traditional ones, like advanced degrees or experience—were irrelevant when superseded by cheerful determination. I was still behaving like a young professional in a world where dues-paying mattered.

In an effort to hype myself up, I developed the theory, however flimsy, that analytics was a natural extension of my liberal arts education. The e-book startup had used the analytics software to track our alpha users through the app, and I had enjoyed looking at some of the data: what our investors were reading, and abandoning; whether or not people read public-domain books with cover art designed by the CPO, which we had added to bolster the library. In a certain light, I tried to convince myself, business analytics could be seen as a form of applied sociology.

The night before the interview, in the privacy of my rental bedroom, I read interviews and puff pieces about the analytics startup's cofounders, now twenty-four and twenty-five years old. According to the tech blogs, they'd just been two underage students with one Silicon Valley internship between them, and a smart, practical, easily pivotable dream of a world driven by the power of big data. This was a dream that greatly appealed to the admissions committee of a renowned seed accelerator in Mountain View, which offered funding and connections in exchange for a 7 percent stake. The accelerator's slogan was an inspirational exhortation to founders to make things people wanted—not, I noted, needed. It boasted a handful of success stories—a grocery-delivery app, a livestreaming site, the home-sharing platform—as well as dozens of failures. The CEO and technical founder had left their college in the Southwest to join the accelerator, then enrolled full-time in the ecosystem.

Several months prior, a tech blog had published an article announcing the analytics startup's first major fund-raising round of ten million dollars. When asked how he would spend the new funding, the CEO made his priorities clear: he would pay the first hundred employees far above market, he said, and spoil current employees to retain them. This was the language of customer acquisition, but I didn't know. I didn't think at all about the stratification, either; how the hundred-and-first employee might feel. I'd never worked anywhere with a hundred people—I'd never worked anywhere with twenty. I'd certainly never worked anywhere that wanted to spoil its employees and had the means to do it. Generous, I thought. I found the tenacity winning.

When I arrived at the analytics startup's headquarters, I was surprised to find that the whole enterprise was peanut-sized. The office, however, was huge—at least seven thousand square feet, with a polished-concrete floor, and mostly unfurnished. About fifteen employees were clustered together at the far end of the room, all gazing deeply into monitors. Some stood at elevated desks, legs spread sturdily, feet cushioned by little rubber mats. Every work space had its own colorful clutter: pots of succulents and other dying plants, anime figurines and stacks of books, bottles of nice liquor. On one was perched an obelisk of empty cans, husks of the same high-caffeine energy drink. The open-plan setup made it look like a classroom. No one there looked over the age of thirty.

I stood in the doorway and counted the women. There were three. They wore jeans and sneakers, oversized cardigans over T-shirts. I had dressed carefully, in a blue shift, heeled boots, and a thin blazer. It was what I always wore to interviews, and I thought it signaled professionalism and seriousness. In publishing, an ensemble like this was nice, but still dowdy enough to be nonthreatening. Inside the startup, I felt like a narc. I shrugged off the blazer as discreetly as possible and stuffed it into my tote bag.

The first interview was with the manager of the Solutions

team, the customer-facing division. He was jolly and hirsute, wearing faded jeans and a company T-shirt that declared I AM DATA DRIVEN. I resisted asking if it needed a hyphen. He sat down in one of the ergonomic desk chairs, leaned back, and bounced lightly, like a baby. Through the glass door of the conference room, on which was taped a handwritten sign designating it THE PENTAGON, I watched a wiry man in a plaid shirt wiggle past on a RipStik, waving one arm for balance and shouting enthusiastically into a golden telephone receiver.

The solutions manager placed his elbows on the table and leaned toward me, explaining that we would be going through a series of questions together so I could demonstrate how I problem-solved. "So," he said, as if he were asking me to let him in on a secret, "how would you calculate the number of people who work for the United States Postal Service?" We sat in silence for a moment. I wouldn't, I thought; I would look it up on the internet. I wondered if perhaps this was actually a test of my tolerance for bullshit and inefficiency—if the sassy response could also be the right one. I had no idea what the solutions manager wanted. Then he handed me a marker and pointed toward the whiteboard. "Why don't you get up on the board and show me how you'd work it out?" he asked. It wasn't a suggestion.

In the four hours that followed, the solutions manager and the wiry man I had earlier seen cruising past, a sales engineer, walked me through a series of questions and puzzles. The sales engineer seemed to be about my age, and had an unaffected drawl and manic, infectious energy. His speech was littered with folksy aphorisms. "Butter my biscuits," he said, when I complimented his oversized belt buckle. "Now we're cooking with gas," he said, teaching me how to reverse a string on the whiteboard.

Both the sales engineer and the solutions manager exclusively referred to the data-analytics software as "the tool." Both of them asked questions that were self-conscious and infuriating. "What's the hardest thing you've ever done?" asked the solutions manager, twisting his wedding ring around and around. "How would you explain the tool to your grandmother?"

"How would you describe the internet to a medieval farmer?" asked the sales engineer, opening and closing the pearl snaps on his shirt, sticking his hand thoughtfully down the back of his own waistband.

Because interviewing at the e-book startup had been breezy and comfortable, I expected the same from the analytics company. No one had warned me that in San Francisco and Silicon Valley interviewing was effectively punitive, more like a hazing ritual than an airtight vetting system. A search-engine giant down in Mountain View was famous for its interview brainteasers, and while it had already denounced the practice, finding it useless as an indicator of future job performance, others insisted on enshrining it as tradition: learning from another company's mistakes took on a new meaning when those mistakes had proved lucrative. Across the Bay Area, applicants were routinely asked questions like "How many square feet of pizza are eaten in the United States every year?" and "How many Ping-Pong balls fit in an airplane?" Some of them, meant to determine whether an interviewee was a culture fit, were dredged in middle-school kitsch. "If you were a superhero, what would your superhero strength be?" asked straight-faced human resources professionals. "When you walk into a room, what's your theme song?" That afternoon, mine was a dirge.

After a few hours, the technical cofounder entered the conference room, looking confidently unprepared. He noted, with an apology, that he hadn't done many interviews before and didn't have any questions to ask. Still, he said, the office manager had slated an hour for our conversation.

This seemed okay: I figured we would talk about the company, I would ask routine follow-up questions, and they would finally let me out, like an elementary-school student, and the city would absorb me and my humiliation. Then the technical cofounder told me that his girlfriend was applying to law school, and he'd been helping her prep. Instead of a conventional interview, he said, he was just going to have me take a section of the LSAT. I searched his baby face to see if he was kidding.

"If it's cool with you, I'm just going to hang out here and check my email," he said, sliding the test across the table and opening a laptop. He set a timer on his phone.

I finished early, ever the overachiever. I checked the test twice. I joked that it was the closest I'd ever come to applying to law school—my mother would be so proud. The technical cofounder shot me a thin smile, slipped the papers under his computer, and left the room.

I sat in his wake, wondering what I was waiting for. There was not a doubt in my mind that I would not get the job. Not only had I surely demonstrated that I was unemployable, but I felt certain I'd been a vivid caricature of the dotty, linty liberal arts major—the antithesis of all that the tech industry stood for.

Still, though the interviews had been inane, they only served to fuel me. Here was a character flaw on parade, my industry origin story: I had always responded well to negging.

I would wonder for years if the analytics startup offered me the job because the entire interview process had revealed a degree of obedience desirable in a customer support representative, and in an employee—if they knew I would ultimately be a push-over, loyal and easily controlled. Eventually, I learned that it was actually just because I had managed a perfect score on the LSAT section they had administered. This knowledge would make me feel simultaneously cocky and displaced, of superior intelligence and crushing foolishness. A part of me had hoped they'd seen something latent and unique, some potential. I was always overthinking things.

The offer included medical and dental coverage, a four-thousand-dollar relocation stipend, and a starting salary of sixty-five thousand dollars a year. The manager informed me that the salary was above market and nonnegotiable. I couldn't fathom being someone who made that much money, much less someone who would try to negotiate for more. With my skill set, or lack thereof, I couldn't believe anyone wanted to pay me that much to do anything.

The solutions manager did not mention equity, and I didn't ask. I did not know that early access to equity was a reason people joined private companies at the startup stage—that it was the only way anyone other than VCs and founders got rich. I did not even know that equity was an option. The company's in-house recruiter would eventually intervene, to recommend that I negotiate to include even a small stake. His rationale was simple: all the other guys had some. No one told me how much it was worth, or how big the pool was, and I did not know to ask.

High on the feeling of being professionally desirable, I told the solutions manager I would sleep on it.

The analytics startup gave me three weeks. Back in Brooklyn, I invited friends over as I packed up the apartment. One evening, after a few drinks, a close friend asked whether I was sure I was making the right decision. I'd enjoyed working in publishing, she reminded me, idly popping bubble wrap between her fingers. Was it perhaps premature to throw in the towel? She promised not to judge if I decided, last minute, not to go. "Mobile analytics," she said, trying on a pair of vintage spectator pumps that I had purchased in the midst of an identity crisis. "What is that? Do you care about it? And customer support—aren't you worried it'll be soul ruining?"

I was worried about a lot of things: loneliness, failure, earthquakes. But I wasn't too worried about my soul. There had always been two sides to my personality. One side was sensible and organized, good at math; appreciative of order, achievement, authority, rules. The other side did everything it could to undermine the first. I behaved as if the first side dominated, but it did not. I wished it did: practicality, I thought, was a safe hedge against failure. It seemed like an easier way to move through the world.

Still, I had trouble admitting to my social group that I was moving across the country solely to work at a startup. It was embarrassing to articulate how excited I was to see what the fuss was about—it seemed, among my countercultural and creative friends, shrewd and cynical to be curious about business. I was selling out. In reality, I was not paying attention: those who understood our cultural moment saw that selling out—corporate positions, partnerships, sponsors—would become our generation's premier aspiration, the best way to get paid.

At the time, though, it was corny to be openly enthusiastic about technology or the internet. For the most part, my friends were late and reluctant adopters. They had accounts on the social network everyone hated, but only used them to RSVP to poetry readings and DIY shows they had no intention of attending. Some defiantly carried flip phones without internet access, preferring to call those of us with desk jobs whenever they were out and needed directions. No one owned an e-reader. As the tides turned digital, my milieu was grounding itself firmly in the embodied, tangible world.

Out of self-protection, I stuck to the narrative that I was moving across the country just to try something new. I had never even lived outside of the tristate area. San Francisco had a great music scene, I said, unconvincingly, to anyone who would listen. It had medical marijuana. Working in analytics would be an experiment in separating my professional life from my personal interests. The startup gig was just a day job, I claimed, something to support me while I was otherwise creatively productive. Maybe I would start the short-story collection I had always wanted to write. Maybe I would take up pottery. I could finally learn bass.

It was easier, in any case, to fabricate a romantic narrative than admit that I was ambitious—that I wanted my life to pick up momentum, go faster.

When I arrived back in San Francisco, with a fresh haircut and two fraying duffel bags, I felt intrepid and pioneering. I did not know that thousands of people had already headed west for a crack at the new American dream, that they had been doing so for years. I was, by many standards, late.

It was a moment of corporate obsequiousness to young men. Tech companies were importing freshly graduated computer science majors from all over the world, putting them up in furnished apartments, paying their cable and internet and cell phone bills, and offering hundred-thousand-dollar signing bonuses as tokens of thanks. The programmers arrived with a flood of nontechnical carpetbaggers: former Ph.D. students and middle-school teachers, public defenders and chamber music singers, financial analysts and assembly-line operators, me.

I had booked another bedroom using the home-sharing platform, this time in the South of Market neighborhood, several blocks from the office. The room was on the garden level of a duplex, adjacent to a concrete patio and accessed through an alley, just past the recycling bins. It was decorated with the same lightweight, self-assembly furniture as my friends' bedrooms back in Brooklyn. The woman who operated the rental was an entrepreneur in the renewable-energy space and described herself as never home.

A few small boxes of my books, bedding, and clothing were already at the analytics startup, stacked in a supply closet. I had been self-conscious about spending down the relocation stipend, wanting to save money for the company. A part of me worried that if I spent too much, the offer would be rescinded. I didn't want my new manager to think I was frivolous. Others had expensed new furniture, meals, weeks of rent, but I didn't know that. I was still operating according to publishing austerity.

The home-sharing platform offered an aspirational fantasy that I appreciated. Across the world, people were squeezing out the last of strangers' toothpaste, picking up strangers' soap in the shower, wiping their noses on strangers' pillowcases. There I was as I had always been, only sleeping in a stranger's bed, fumbling to replace a stranger's spring-loaded toilet-paper holder, ordering sweaters off a stranger's Wi-Fi network. I liked examining someone else's product selections, judging their clutter. I wasn't thinking about how the home-sharing platform might also be driving up rents, displacing residents, or undermining the very authenticity that it purported to sell. Mostly, the fact that it functioned, and nobody had murdered me, seemed like a miracle.

I had given myself a few days to get adjusted before starting the job. In the mornings, I bought coffee at a laundromat, consulted a crowdsourced reviewing app to find something to eat, and returned to my bedroom to spend the rest of the day reading technical documentation for the analytics software and panicking. The documentation was indecipherable to me. I didn't know what an API was, or how to use one. I didn't know

how I would possibly provide technical support to engineers—
I couldn't even fake it.

The night before my first day of work, too unmoored and
overwhelmed to sleep, I scrolled through previous guests' reviews of my room and realized that the apartment was owned by
one of the founders of the home-sharing platform. I looked up
the founder's name and read an interview in which he detailed
how designers could follow in his footsteps and become entrepreneurs. He called them "designpreneurs." I watched a video
of him delivering the keynote at a tech conference, breathing
excitedly into the mic. I learned that he and his two cofounders
had raised over a hundred million dollars, and investors were
desperate to give them more.

I looked around me at the blank walls, the closet door
tilted on its hinges, the bars on the window, eager to identify
hints of his success. But the designpreneur hadn't slept in
the room for years. He had moved into a gleaming, art-filled
warehouse conversion close to his office. He'd left nothing
behind.

The analytics startup made a pickax-during-the-Gold-Rush
product, the kind venture capitalists loved to get behind. History
saw the Gold Rush as a cautionary tale, but in Silicon Valley,
people used its metaphors proudly, provided they were on the
right side of things. Pickaxes were usually business-to-business
products. Infrastructure, not services. Just as startups in New
York were eager to build off their city's existing cultural legacy,
by creating services for media and finance—or, more com-
monly, creating sleek interfaces to sell things that would require
more time, money, energy, or taste to buy elsewhere—the same
was true of the Bay Area, where software engineers sought to

usurp older technology companies by building tools for other software engineers.

It was the era of big data, complex data sets facilitated by exponentially faster computer processing power and stored, fashionably, in the cloud. Big data encompassed industries: science, medicine, farming, education, policing, surveillance. The right findings could be golden, inspiring new products or revealing user psychology, or engendering ingenious, hypertargeted advertising campaigns.

Not everyone knew what they needed from big data, but everyone knew that they needed it. Just the prospect incited lust in product managers, advertising executives, and stock-market speculators. Data collection and retention were unregulated. Investors salivated over predictive analytics, the lucrative potential of steroidal pattern-matching, and the prospect of bringing machine-learning algorithms to the masses—or, at least, to Fortune 500 companies. Transparency for the masses wasn't ideal: better that the masses not see what companies in the data space had on them.

The analytics startup wasn't disrupting anything so much as unseating big-data incumbents: slow-moving corporate behemoths whose products were technically unsophisticated and bore distinctly nineties user interfaces. The startup not only enabled other companies to collect customized data on their users' behavior without having to write much code or pay for storage, but it also offered ways to analyze that data in colorful, dynamic dashboards. The cofounders had prioritized aesthetics and hired two graphic designers off the bat: men with signature hairstyles and large followings on a social network for people who referred to themselves as creatives and got excited about things like font sizing and hero images. In general, it was hard to say what, exactly, the designers did all day, but the dashboards were both friendly and elegant. The software looked especially pleasing, trustworthy, airtight. Good interface design was like magic, or religion: it cultivated the mass suspension of disbelief.

I had no qualms about disrupting extant corporations in the big-data space, no inherited nostalgia or fondness for business. I liked the underdog. I liked the idea of working for two kids younger than I was, who had dropped out of college and were upending the script for success. It was thrilling, in that sense, to see a couple of twentysomethings go up against middle-aged leaders of industry. It looked like they could win.

I was employee number twenty, and the fourth woman. Prior to my arrival, the Solutions team—four men, including the manager—had handled customer tickets themselves, attacking the support queue in shifts at the end of the workday, relaying the responsibility to avoid consecutive office-bound midnights. This strategy was effective for a while, but the user base was ballooning. The men couldn't sustain the practice; they had their own jobs to do. They rearranged their desktop belongings and cleared a space for me.

The men on the Solutions team weren't like the men from the e-book startup. They were weirder, wilder, funnier, harder to keep up with. They wore Australian work boots and flannel and durable, recycled polyester athletic vests, drank energy shots in the late afternoon and popped vitamin D in the mornings to stay focused and alert. They chewed powdered Swedish tobacco, packing it juicily behind their gums. Deep house and EDM leaked from their oversized headphones. At team gatherings they drank whiskey, neat, and, the following mornings, were prone to pounding a viscous liquid jacked up with electrolytes—sold as a remedy for small children with diarrhea—to flush away their hangovers. They had gone to top-tier private colleges and were fluent in the jargon of media studies and literary theory. They reminded me of my friends who had left San Francisco, but more adaptable and opportunistic, happier.

The solutions manager assigned me an onboarding buddy, Noah, a curly-haired twenty-six-year-old with a forearm tattoo in Sanskrit and a wardrobe of workman's jackets and soft fleeces. Noah was warm and loquacious, animated, handsome. He struck me as the kind of person who would invite women over to get stoned and look at art books and listen to Brian Eno, and then actually spend the night doing that. I had gone to college with men like this: men who would comfortably sit on the floor with their backs against the bed, men who self-identified as feminists and would never make the first move. I could immediately picture him making seitan stir-fry, suggesting a hike in the rain. Showing up in an emergency and thinking he knew exactly what to do. Noah spoke in absolutes and in the language of psychoanalysis, offering definitive narratives for everyone, everything. I had the uneasy feeling that he could persuade me to do anything: bike across America; join a cult.

Noah and I spent my first few weeks in various corners of the office, carting around an overflowing bowl of trail mix and a rolling whiteboard, on which he patiently diagrammed how cookie tracking worked, how data was sent server-side, how to send an HTTP request, how to prevent a race condition. He was patient and encouraging, and made direct eye contact as we pushed through problem sets of hypothetical customer questions, various scenarios in which the software—or, more realistically, the user—had a meltdown.

The product was actually deeply technical, though the company talked up its usability. The amount of information I needed to absorb, to be even marginally helpful to our customers, was intimidating. The learning curve looked unconquerable. Noah gave me homework and pep talks. He told me not to worry. Our teammates handed me beers in the late afternoon, and were confident and reassuring that I, too, would eventually scale up. I trusted them entirely.

I was happy; I was learning. For the first time in my professional life, I was not responsible for making anyone coffee. Instead, I was solving problems. My job involved surveying strangers' codebases and telling them where they'd gone wrong in integrating our product with theirs, and how to fix it. The first time I looked at a block of code and understood what was happening, I felt like nothing less than a genius.

It did not take long for me to understand the fetish for big data. Data sets were mesmerizing: digital streams of human behavior, answers to questions I didn't know I had. There was more every second. Our servers, and the company's bank account, absorbed this unstoppable wave.

Our bread and butter was engagement: actions that demonstrated the ways users were interacting with a product. This was a turn away from the long-running industry standard, which prioritized metrics like page views and time on site, metrics that the CEO called bullshit. Engagement, he said, was distinguished from the bullshit because it was actionable. Engagement generated a feedback loop between the user and the company. User behavior could dictate product managers' decisions. These insights would be fed back into an app or website, to dictate or predict subsequent user behavior.

The software was flexible, intended to function as easily for fitness trackers or payment processors as for photo-editing and ride-sharing apps. It could be integrated into online boutiques, digital megamalls, banks, social networks, streaming and gaming websites. It gathered data for platforms that enabled people to book flights or hotels or restaurant reservations or wedding venues; platforms for buying a house or finding a house cleaner, ordering takeout or arranging a date. Engineers and data scientists and product managers would inject snippets of our code into their own codebases, specify which behaviors they wanted to track, and begin collecting data immediately. Anything an app or website's users did—tap a button, take a photograph, send a payment, swipe right, enter text—could be recorded in real time, stored, aggregated, and analyzed in those beautiful dashboards. Whenever I explained it to friends, I sounded like a podcast ad.

Depending on the metadata, users' actions could be scrutinized down to the bone, at the most granular level imaginable. Data could be segmented by anything an app collected—age, gender, political affiliation, hair color, dietary restrictions, body weight, income bracket, favorite movies, education, kinks, proclivities—plus some IP-based defaults, like country, city, cell phone carrier, device type, and a unique device identification code. If women in Boise were using an exercise app primarily between the hours of nine and eleven in the morning—only once a month, mostly on Sunday, and for an average of twenty-nine minutes—the software could know. If people on a dating website were messaging everyone within walking distance who practiced yoga, trimmed their pubic hair, and were usually monogamous but looking for a threesome during a stint in New Orleans, the software could know that, too. All customers had to do was run a report; all they had to do was ask.

We also offered a secondary product, a people-analytics tool, for which some customers paid extra. The people-analytics tool stored individual profiles of users on those customers' platforms. These contained streams of personalized, searchable activity, as well as any identifying metadata. The point of this tool was to facilitate outreach based on behavior, and incentivize re-engagement. An e-commerce store could search its own database to see which men, exactly, were filling online shopping carts with razor blades and beard oil but never checking out, and send those men an email, offering discounts or simply a passive-aggressive reminder that it might be time to shave. A food-delivery app, upon registering that a user had ordered a paleo TV tray six nights in a row, might trigger an in-app pop-up suggesting she try a carbohydrate. An exercise app could identify that a user had stopped a workout at the burpee section and automatically send a push notification asking him if he was still alive.

The tool was free to use to a certain threshold, after which data was metered. If our customer companies acquired more users of their own, their volume of data would increase, and their monthly invoices would spike accordingly. This meant the tool was inherently lucrative, because every company wanted to grow. The underlying assumption was that if our customers were bringing on more users, they should also be bringing in more money; that revenue and usage were linked.

This turned out to be generous. Many startups didn't have a revenue model to begin with, optimizing instead for market penetration. In these cases, venture capital served as a placeholder for profit: companies acquired more users without bringing in more money, as if they were simply an intermediary between us and their investors' bank accounts. Our payment structure was straightforward, simple, canny. It would have been logical, too, if logic—or basic economics—had any governance over the venture-backed ecosystem.

To do my job effectively, I had to be able to see customers' code, as well as their dashboards. This was true of anyone in a customer-facing role; it was almost impossible to solve users' problems if the problems weren't in front of us. The simplest way for the analytics startup to achieve this was by granting those of us on the Solutions team access to all of our customers' data sets: to see the tool as if we were logged in to any given user's account, to experience our product through their eyes.

Some called this setting God Mode. It wasn't our customers' payment, contact, and organizational information—though we could see that, too, if we needed to—but the actual data sets that they collected on their own users. This was a privileged vantage point from which to observe the tech industry, and we tried not to talk about it. "We're not just selling jeans to miners," Noah said. "We're doing everyone's laundry."

God Mode was a business education. Engagement metrics could tell the story of a startup's entire life span. Startups rumored to be rocket ships sputtered to get off the ground. Gaming apps spiked and flamed out within weeks. The descent into obsolescence was almost always broken by cushions of venture capital, but we could see the direction things would go.

We all knew that internal permissions, limiting what we could see of customer data sets, would come eventually. We also knew, at least for the time being, that it wasn't a priority for our Engineering team. This level of employee access was normal for the industry—common for small, new startups whose engineers were overextended. Employees at ride-sharing startups,

I'd heard, could search customers' ride histories, tracking the travel patterns of celebrities and politicians. Even the social network everyone hated had its own version of God Mode: early employees had been granted access to users' private activity and passwords. Permissioning was effectively a rite of passage. It was a concession to the demands of growth.

Besides, early employees were trusted like family. It was assumed we would only look at our customers' data sets out of necessity, and only when requested by customers themselves; that we would not, under any circumstances, look up individual profiles of our lovers and family members and coworkers in the data sets belonging to dating apps and shopping services and fitness trackers and travel sites. We would not, out of sociological curiosity, surf through data sets of neighborhood-watch platforms and online programs for Christian men trying to kick their masturbation habits. We would not pry.

It was assumed that we wouldn't check back on past employers to see how they were faring without us. It was assumed we would never discuss the glaring inconsistencies between the public narratives spun around our startup customers and the stories that their data told: if we were to read breathless, frothy tech-blog coverage about companies we suspected were failing, we would only smile and close the tab. It was assumed that if we had a publicly traded company using our software—and, if so moved, could chart the overall health of that public company based on its data set, or build out predictive models of when its overall value might grow or recede—we would resist buying or selling its stock.

Our tiny company of twentysomethings operated on good faith. If good faith failed, there was a thorough audit log of all employee behavior: the founders had implemented a product on our own back end, which tracked the customer data sets we looked at and the specific reports we ran. But nobody ever used the words "insider trading." Nobody had a press contact. There was no policy on leaks. Not that we needed one—we were all, as the CEO liked to remind us, Down for the Cause.

... ...
... ...
... ...
... ...

San Francisco was an underdog city struggling to absorb an influx of aspiring alphas. It had long been a haven for hippies and queers, artists and activists, Burners and leather daddies, the disenfranchised and the weird. It also had a historically corrupt government, and a housing market built atop racist urban-renewal policies—real estate values had benefited as much from redlining as from discriminatory zoning practices and midcentury internment camps—but these narratives, along with the reality that an entire generation had been prematurely lost to AIDS, undercut its reputation as a mecca for the free and freakish, people on the fringe. The city, trapped in nostalgia for its own mythology, stuck in a hallucination of a halcyon past, had not quite caught up to the newfound momentum of tech's dark triad: capital, power, and a bland, overcorrected, heterosexual masculinity.

It was a strange place for young and moneyed futurists. In the absence of vibrant cultural institutions, the pleasure center of the industry might have just been exercise: people courted the sublime on trail runs and day hikes, glamped in Marin and

rented chalets in Tahoe. They dressed for work as if embarking on an alpine expedition: high-performance down jackets
and foul-weather shells, backpacks with decorative carabi-
ners. They looked ready to gather kindling and build a lean-to,
not make sales calls and open pull-requests from climate-
controlled open-plan offices. They looked in costume to LARP
their weekend selves.

The culture these inhabitants sought and fostered was
lifestyle. They engaged with their new home by rating it.
Crowdsourced reviewing apps provided opportunities to assign
anything a grade: dim sum, playgrounds, hiking trails. Founders went out to eat and confirmed that the food tasted exactly
how other reviewers promised it would; they posted redundant
photographs of plated appetizers and meticulous restaurant-
scapes. They pursued authenticity without realizing that the
most authentic thing about the city was, at this moment in
time, them.

The city's passive-aggressive, progressive, permissive politics tended to rankle transplants, but tech's self-appointed representatives weren't for everyone, either. Every three months
a different engineer or aspiring entrepreneur, new to the city,
would post a screed on a blogging platform with no revenue
model. He would excoriate the poor for clinging to rent control and driving up condo prices, or excoriate the tent cities by
the freeway for being an eyesore. He would suggest monetizing homeless people by turning them into Wi-Fi hotspots. He
would lambaste the weak local sports teams, the abundance
of bicyclists, the fog. *Like a woman who is constantly PMSing*,
a twenty-three-year-old founder of a crowdfunding platform
wrote about the climate. The extension of casual misogyny to
weather was creative, but the digital ambassadors didn't seem
to like actual women, either: they whined that the women in San

Francisco were fives, not tens, and whined that there weren't enough of them.

Like most of the larger, older, serious hardware corporations, the major internet upstarts had hunkered down on the suburban Peninsula, thirty miles south. Their campuses offered candy stores and rock-climbing gyms, bike-repair shops and doctors' offices, gourmet cafeterias and hair salons, nutritionists and day cares. They offered no reason to ever leave. The campuses were accessible by public transportation, but public transportation did not offer Wi-Fi. Every weekday, private shuttles looped through the city's residential neighborhoods, pausing at public bus stops to pick up commuters.

The commuters wore corporate identification badges clipped to their belt loops or draped on top of their jackets, like children trying not to get lost in a mall. They stood in line for the shuttles with their backpacks and reusable coffee cups; some slung bags of dirty laundry over their shoulders. They looked tired, resigned, sheepish. Mostly, they looked at their phones.

Transplanted startup workers bemoaned the transit infrastructure, an old system riddled with inefficiencies that shut down almost entirely at midnight—not that anyone making a midlevel tech salary was taking the bus. A glut of transportation apps had sprung up to replace San Francisco's poky streetcars and unreliable taxi fleet. The largest was an on-demand ride-sharing startup, a company committed to domination at all costs, including profitability.

The ride-sharing startup's main competitor had a near-identical business model but much cuter branding. The cute competitor required its drivers—contract laborers commandeering their own personal vehicles—to hook large fuchsia mustaches, made of synthetic fur, to their grilles and greet passengers with a fist bump. Improbably, this worked. The company knew its audience: San Franciscans, living in neighborhoods where every other storefront had a pun in its name, were corny.

I abandoned my expectations for how cities should be. Bars and cafés opened late and closed early; traffic seemed to slide backward, downhill. The city dealt in improbable couplings. A pay-as-you-wish yoga studio shared a creaky walk-up with the headquarters of an encrypted-communications platform. A bodega selling loosies sat below an anarchistic hacker space. The older office buildings, regal and unkempt with marble floors and peeling paint, housed orthodontists and rare-book dealers alongside four-person companies trying to gamify human resources or commoditize meditation. Data scientists smoked weed in Dolores Park with Hula-Hoopers and blissed-out suburban teenagers. The independent movie theaters played ads for networked appliances and B2B software before projecting seventies cult classics. Even racks at the dry cleaner suggested a city in transition: starched police uniforms and synthetic neon furs, sheathed in plastic, hung beside custom-made suits and machine-washable pullovers.

Homeless encampments sprouted in the shadows of luxury developments. People slept and shat and shot up in the train stations, lying beneath advertisements for fast fashion and productivity apps, as waves of commuters stepped delicately around them. I woke up one morning to the sound of someone howling for mercy on the corner of my block: a woman screaming bloody murder, dragging one leg, wearing nothing but a torn T-shirt emblazoned with the logo for a multinational consumer-electronics company.

This concentration of public pain was new to me, unsettling. I had never seen such a shameful juxtaposition of blatant suffering and affluent idealism. It was a well-publicized disparity, but one I had underestimated. As a New Yorker, I had thought I was

prepared. I thought I'd seen it all. I felt humbled and naïve—
and guilty, all the time.

I moved into an apartment in the Castro, joining a man and a
woman in their late twenties, roommates who had wiggled their
way onto a hand-me-down lease. They were tech workers, too.
The woman worked as a midlevel product manager at the social
network everyone hated; the man as a data scientist at a struggling solar-energy startup. They were both endurance runners;
the data scientist kept a road bike in his bedroom. They had
no body fat. They had no art in the apartment, either. On the
refrigerator was an impressive collection of novelty magnets
arranged in a perfect grid.

The apartment was gigantic, a duplex with two living rooms
and a view of the bay. Both roommates claimed they wanted to
live independently but couldn't abandon the rent control. With
a combined household income that easily topped four hundred thousand dollars—not including the product manager's
stock—we were not people for whom rent control was intended,
but there we were. When I signed a sublease in exchange for the
keys, my new roommates congratulated me on my good luck.

I got along better with the product manager, though we
occupied different spaces: I was in the startup world, land of
perpetual youth, and she was an adult like any other, navigating
a corporation, acting the part, negotiating for her place. She
was classically trained in violin and collected leather-bound
antique books, like a Chekhov character. I felt uncultured by
comparison, with my colorful contemporary paperbacks and
penchant for overwrought indie rock. She seemed to find me
amusing, maybe a little pitiable. I admired and did not understand her. Mostly, we talked about exercise.

The bedroom I sublet had an air mattress and a fire escape. One by one, I moved my boxes out of the startup's supply closet. I stacked the books on the floor, unrolled a camping blanket onto the bed, hung my blouses and wrap dresses in the closet. My clothes looked like they belonged to someone else, probably because they did. After a few weeks, I folded them back up and sent them to a publishing friend in New York, who still dressed up for the other women in her office.

The fire escape offered a private passage to the roof, and from time to time I would climb up to take stock. I would gaze out over the pastel Victorians, the rustling magnolia trees, the fog rushing over the hills, the container ships skimming the bay. Every so often, I felt a wave of affection for San Francisco, a thrill like hope—a sense, however small, that it could eventually become home.

When the product manager turned thirty, she hosted a wine and cheese party at our apartment. The data scientist and I were invited. I marked it on my calendar, as if I would forget.

The product manager's friends arrived promptly, in cocktail attire. She was intimidating in black silk. Hundreds of dollars' worth of cheese had been procured, and classical music streamed through the house. A man opened a bottle of champagne, which he reassured us was from France. People clapped when the cork popped.

Feeling like a child at my parents' party, I sent myself to my room, locked the door, and changed out of work clothes—baggy sweater, high-waisted jeans—and into a very tight dress. I had gained five, eight, ten pounds in trail mix. When I reentered the living room, I sucked in my stomach and slid between people's backs, looking for a conversation. On the couch, two men in suit jackets expounded on opportunities in cannabis. Everyone seemed very comfortable and nobody talked to me. They tilted their wineglasses at the correct angle; they dusted crumbs off their palms with grace. The word I heard the most was "revenue." Maybe "strategy."

This was the nascent neomillionaire class, I realized. They weren't all rich, not yet, but they were right on track. My coworkers were also aspiring, but they had a different style. Not one of them would be caught dead wearing a tailored suit to a house party.

I wound up on the roof with a cluster of men. In the distance was the tip of the famous rainbow flag on Castro Street, whipping. I felt a twist of homesickness, the jolt of being three thousand miles away from my mother.

"We're looking to buy in Oakland," one of the men was saying.

"Too dangerous," said another. "My wife would never go for it."

"Of course not," replied the first, absently swirling his wine. "But you don't buy to live there."

By the time the last guest filtered out, I was already in leggings and a sweatshirt, half-drunk and cleaning: scooping up cheese rinds, rinsing plastic glasses, sneaking slices of chocolate cake with damp hands. The product manager came to say good night, and she was beautiful: tipsy but not toasted, radiant with absorbed goodwill. She repaired to her room with her boyfriend. From down the hall, I could hear them as they quietly undressed, eased into bed, and turned over into sleep.

Most nights, I worked late. The neighborhood around the office emptied out after dark. An off-price department store glowed on the corner. Men in shredded pants shuffled in front of the train station, shouting down nobody.

I downloaded the ride-sharing apps that everyone had said I would want, but which I had resisted. I found the premise creepy: I had never wanted to get into strangers' cars, hated hitchhiking, had been told my entire life never to do so. Being chauffeured by other adults in their own vehicles didn't seem luxurious to me, it looked like carpooling. Carpooling, however, was meant to be a social good with an environmental benefit. It seemed cynical and backward to pay a private company to brute-force carpooling by putting more cars on the road.

But the buses had delays and broke down; the light rail back to the Castro came every forty minutes. A car, by contrast, was a tunnel to home. I found myself ducking into strangers' sedans on a nightly basis, meekly extending my fist for a tap, chattering on mindlessly from the back seat. Clutching my keys, crossing my fingers.

As part of the onboarding process, the operations manager set me up on lunch dates with coworkers from across the company. I went out with an account manager whose desk faced mine in the cluster. He often air-golfed, perfecting his swing, while on the phone with customers. He called the Mission "the Mish," but I liked him a lot. He was easy to talk to; he was easy to talk to for a living.

The account manager and I procured large, sloppy sandwiches and sat down in a plaza between two hotels. We gazed out at the underdressed tourists. I asked how he had chosen to work at the analytics startup—he'd studied history, after all. It wasn't a major I associated with upselling. "Come on," he said. "I heard there were a bunch of twentysomethings crushing it in the Valley. How often does that happen?"

Relatively often, I had assumed. The plaza was full of people who looked just like us: white and young and exhausted, coasting on caffeine and simple carbohydrates. The previous year, a thirteen-person startup, the maker of a photo-sharing app, had been acquired for a billion dollars by the social network everyone hated. Their office was three blocks away. "This is a get-rich-quick scheme," the account manager said. "We built a tool that's, what, five, ten years in the future? Nobody has ever seen something like this before. The product practically sells itself."

I had not fully grasped how rare the analytics startup was. Ninety-five percent of startups tanked. We weren't just beating the odds; we were soaring past them. This was what everyone who trekked out to the Bay Area wanted, but it was not actually supposed to happen. The CEO of the e-book startup had been right: the analytics startup was a rocket ship. Despite its size and age, the company was already well regarded and legitimate, marked to become a unicorn. We were hurtling toward a billion-dollar valuation. Our revenue soared every month. We were winning, and we would be rich.

"This company is going to be worth a gajillion dollars," the account manager said, taking a bite of potato salad. "We're ripping up and to the right. We have the best and the brightest. We're on an immutable path toward success. We're all just fucking ready to give whatever needs to be given to make this thing happen. All anyone is asking is for us to pour our hearts and souls into this unstoppable behemoth." He drained his iced coffee. "Frankly," he said, "I think it's a pretty good bargain."

I went on another arranged lunch, with the CTO. We had never spoken; I didn't know what to expect. According to my teammates, the CTO was brilliant and difficult. An autodidact, he hadn't graduated high school, but he could single-handedly design the sort of complex database infrastructure that, elsewhere, would have taken a team of experienced computer scientists. I didn't know whether this was hyperbolic, but it didn't matter: he was the only employee to whom the founders deferred. This wasn't just programmer supremacy, despite its popularity. He was the only one who really understood the core technology. The company wouldn't exist without him.

The CTO was in his early thirties, with untended facial stubble and beautiful, wide-set eyes. He often smelled like menthols. While the other engineers had condos in the Marina or renovated Victorian apartments lining Dolores Park, he lived in the Tenderloin, a high-crime neighborhood with a concentration of SROs and open-air drug markets—*on purpose*, Noah had once said, eyebrows raised in admiration. The CTO shuffled into the office every afternoon with headphones on, holding a paper cup of coffee and avoiding eye contact. He almost always wore a T-shirt with the company logo on it and an unbranded navy-blue hoodie.

We ordered salads at a faux-French café in the financial district and sat at a rickety table outside, watching the midday stream of men with briefcases and women in shift dresses. They looked so much older than we did, in their inoffensive textiles and fake alligator loafers. They looked straight out of another era, like the nineties. I wondered how we looked to them: two round-cheeked slobs in T-shirts and sneakers, eating slices of grilled chicken like teenage miscreants with a stolen credit card. I nudged my backpack under the table, out of view.

My coworkers had warned me that the CTO was inscrutable and reticent, but after a few minutes I wondered how hard any of them had tried. I was surprised to find that he had a dark, sarcastic sense of humor. We had more in common than I would have guessed: compulsive reading habits; insomnia. While I usually spent sleepless nights staring at the ceiling and worry-

ing about my loved ones' mortality, he worked on programming
side projects. Sometimes he just passed the time between midnight and noon playing a long-haul trucking simulator. It was
calming, he said. There was a digital CB radio through which
he could communicate with other players. I pictured him whis-
pering into it in the dark.

The thought of him awake at three in the morning, barrel-
ing down a digital highway, fiddling with the controls in a digital cab, patching through to strangers, made me wonder how
he would fare in Brooklyn, around people who might appreciate
or encourage his curiosity about things other than code. I
still clung, condescendingly, to the conceit that art could be an
existential curative. That music or literature was all anyone
was ever missing. That somehow these pursuits were more
genuine, more fulfilling than software. I didn't consider that
perhaps he liked his life—that he wanted it to look in no way
like the one I had left.

As we walked back to the office, I told him about my friends
in New York, and how they didn't seem to understand the appeal of working in technology. In the elevator, we joked about
building an app that might interest them, one that would algo-
rithmically suggest pairings of cocktail recipes and literature,
according to a given book's mood, era, and themes. I returned
to my desk and didn't think about it again—until the following
afternoon, when the CTO messaged me in the company chat
room and told me he had built it.

The startup hosted a monthly salon for the data curious, a catered happy hour with presentations from product managers and
engineers, sourced from our customer list, about how to use an-

alytics to run A/B tests, or growth-hack, or monitor user flows. Though I had loved going to publishing parties, where chatty editorial assistants quickly eschewed professional networking to gossip and gripe, nibble on stale pretzels and drugstore holiday cookies, and drink too much cheap wine—which always gave these evenings a coursing undercurrent of peculiar sexual energy—I had not been to tech networking events in either New York or San Francisco. I was curious, the day of my first big-data happy hour, about who would voluntarily spend their evening in someone else's office listening to a sponsored presentation about mobile analytics.

The event was packed. Almost all the attendees were young men in startup twinsets, branded hoodies unzipped to reveal T-shirts with the same logo. Not that I could judge—we all wore our own branded T-shirts, most of them snatched from the supply closet, creases from the folds still visible. A small team of caterers worked furiously in the kitchen, arranging platters of cheese and replenishing coolers with beer and bottles of local white wine. There was a six-pack of root beer for the solutions manager, who was Mormon. I found the root beer moving.

The men roamed in clusters, like college freshmen during orientation week. They stood near our cloth-covered lunch tables and loaded compostable plates with charcuterie and fruit, crudités and hors d'oeuvres: lamb sliders, steamed barbecue-pork buns, tiny shrimp spring rolls. There was not a coursing undercurrent of peculiar sexual energy, or any sexual energy at all; everything was straightforward, up front. The attendees were clear about what they wanted, which was for their companies to grow. They were excited to talk about their startups, and all small talk was prelude to a pitch. I was guilty of this, too: I was proud of where I worked, and we badly needed to hire.

Our team was penned off in a corner of the office, at a cluster of tables marked with a sign that read SOLUTIONS ZONE. I stood in the Zone and felt powerful. Because the products of our labor were intangible, meeting customers felt amazing—validating. They approached, gave us their company names, and asked for help running reports. We never asked for their corporate ID cards or any sort of validation, and none of them ever questioned why it was so easy for us to pull up their data sets. Their companies had customer-support teams, too.

The presentation that evening was top-shelf: a fireside chat between two venture capitalists. There wasn't an actual fire, but the VCs looked sweaty, close to pitting out. Even from the back row, the office felt moist. I'd never been in a room with so few women, so much money, and so many people champing at the bit to get a taste. It was like watching two ATMs in conversation. "I want big data on men talking about big data," I whispered to one of the engineers, who ignored me.

After the event, we traveled in a group to a bar around the corner. The bar was subterranean and meant to look like a speakeasy, with heavy velvet curtains, a live jazz band, and bartenders who referred to themselves as mixologists. The faux speakeasy, on the edge of a neighborhood filled with paperless offices, was newspaper themed. Newsprint that looked like it had been soaked in black tea lined the walls. Typewriters were scattered about as decorative objects.

My coworkers looked glossy, exhausted, proud. They took shots, jostled against each other, jockeyed for the CEO's attention. I found myself at a two-top with him, briefly, drinking something heavily garnished with mint. "I want you to eventually lead Support," the CEO said, leaning in. "We need more women in leadership roles." I basked in his attention. When I finished my drink, I let the ice melt, and then I drank that, too. I didn't think to mention that if he wanted more women in leadership roles, perhaps we should start by hiring more women. I didn't note that even if we did hire more women, there were elements of our office culture that women might find uncomfortable. Instead, I told him I would do whatever he needed.

Later, I stood in line for the bathroom behind two women in heels and day-to-night dresses. They looked around my age, but polished—shinier. They looked like the sort of woman I had wanted, and failed, to become back in publishing: self-possessed, socially graceful, manicured. They were probably having a different kind of night. The three of us leaned against the tiled wall and pawed our devices. My inbox was full of customer emails. I tried not to look down at my untucked shirt and tennis sneakers, my hips lapping over the lip of my jeans, the name tag on my chest that read SOLUTIONS! I tried not to imagine myself in their shoes.

When I reentered the bar, thankful for the dim light, I realized nobody else in our group had bothered to change before leaving the office, either. Like campers on a field trip, we were all still wearing our company T-shirts. I AM DATA DRIVEN, our chests announced to the world.

Every Tuesday, at exactly noon, over a hundred synchronized sirens wailed across San Francisco, a test of the city's emergency warning system. The sirens also signaled, at the analytics startup, that it was time for our weekly all-hands. The most obedient of us would perch on the two sofas in the middle of the office, and the rest would roll over in their desk chairs, flanking the CEO in a semicircle like children at a progressive kindergarten.

At the start of each meeting, the operations manager distributed packets containing metrics and updates from across the company: sales numbers, new signups, deals closed. We were all privy to high-level details and minutiae, from the names and progress of job candidates to projected revenue. This panoramic view of the business meant individual contributions were noticeable; it felt good to identify and measure our impact. At the end of the meeting, the packets were gathered, and later shredded.

The meeting's highlight was always the CEO, who would debrief us on the financial health of the company, our product road map, his big-picture plans. As was trendy in the ecosystem, we embraced transparency. Truly important decisions were likely made in the Pentagon, or in back-channel chat rooms, but it still felt good to be included.

We were doing well—we were always doing well. In a culture where profitability was a bragging right, we had plenty to be smug about. Our revenue graphs looked like cartoons of revenue graphs. The engineers had built an internal website where we could watch the money come in, in real time. The message was clear, and intoxicating: society valued our contributions and, by extension, us. An IPO seemed not just inevitable but imminent.

Even so, the enemy of a successful startup was complacency. To combat this, the CEO liked to instill fear. He was not a formidable physical presence—he had gelled, spiky hair; he was slight; he often wore a green jacket indoors, presumably to fight the chill—but he could scare the hell out of us. He spoke in military terms. "We are at war," he would say, standing in front of us with his arms crossed and his jaw tensed. Across the world, Syria and Iraq and Israel raged. We were at war with competitors, for market share. We would look down at our bottles of kombucha or orange juice and nod along gravely.

The CEO was not especially inspirational, but he was impressive. It wasn't just that he was the most powerful person in the room—though he was, of course, always the most powerful person in the room. Everything he touched seemed to turn to gold. When he identified any one of us as having done something good, a rare occurrence, it was deeply gratifying. We were desperate to please him. We never stopped moving. We were Down for the Cause.

Down for the Cause: the phrase was in our job listings and our internal communications. It meant putting the company first, and was the highest form of praise. The holy grail was being thanked by the CEO in person—or, better yet, in the company chat room—for being DFTC. This happened, from time to time, if one of us did something especially useful outside of our job description. If he was in the right mood. If we were lucky.

Camaraderie came easy. The office was big enough to keep a wide berth if we wanted one, but we stayed close. We all knew who was hungover. We all knew if someone was suffering from stress-induced IBS. We abided by what we jokingly called the ass-in-chair metric: our presence was proof. Slacking off was not an option. If someone was missing, something was wrong. Research showed little correlation between productivity and extended working hours, but the tech industry thrived on the idea of its own exceptionalism; the data did not apply to us.

Besides, we were having fun. We were circumventing the fussiness and protocol of the corporate world: there was always an opportunity to accelerate straight into management, like skipping a grade, skipping three. We dressed however we wanted. We were forgiven our quirks. As long as we were productive, we could be ourselves.

Work had wedged its way into our identities. We were the company; the company was us. Small failures and major successes were equally reflective of our personal inadequacies or individual brilliance. Momentum was intoxicating, as was the feeling that we were all indispensable. Whenever we saw a stranger at the gym wearing a T-shirt with our logo on it, whenever we were mentioned on social media or on a client's blog, whenever we received a positive support ticket, we shared it in the company chat room and we felt proud, genuinely proud.

•

I began wearing flannel. I bought Australian work boots and biked to work in them, sweating. I incorporated B vitamins into my regimen and felt more awake, more cheerful. I began dipping into EDM. It was a vestige of Burning Man that never went out of season in the Bay Area, like ecstatic dance or LED-studded sculptures or psychedelic leggings.

Listening to EDM while I worked gave me delusions of grandeur, but it kept me in a rhythm. It was the genre of my generation: the music of video games and computer effects, the music of the twenty-four-hour hustle, the music of proudly selling out. It was decadent and cheaply made, the music of ahistory, or globalization—or maybe nihilism, but fun. It made me feel like I had just railed cocaine, except happy. It made me feel like I was going somewhere.

Was this what it felt like to hurtle through the world in a state of pure confidence, I wondered, pressing my fingers to my temples—was this what it was like to be a man? The sheer ecstasy of the drop made everything around me feel like part of a running-shoe ad or a luxury car commercial, though I couldn't imagine driving to EDM, or even online shopping. I couldn't imagine playing it for my parents. I would lean against my standing desk and dance while pounding out emails, nodding in solidarity with the rest of the team. My feet may as well have been turning the world.

My teammates were all skilled at maneuvering the RipStiks. They glided across the office, twisting and dipping with laptops in hand, taking customer calls on their personal cell phones, shuttling from desk to kitchen to conference room.

Mastering the RipStik was a rite of passage, and I could not do it. After a few weeks of trying, I ordered a tiny skateboard off the internet, a neon green piece of plastic with four wheels that looked coolest when it wasn't being ridden. I came into the office over the weekend to practice on the skateboard, perfecting my balance. It was fast, dangerously so. Mostly I put it under my standing desk and then got on board, rocking back and forth as I worked.

Our core users were programmers and data scientists, almost all of whom, by nature of the industry, were men. I grew comfortable talking to them about the technology without really understanding the technology itself. I found myself confidently discussing cookies, data mapping, the difference between server-side and client-side. Just add logic, I advised cheerfully. This meant nothing to me but generally resonated with engineers.

Twice a week, I hosted live, instructional webinars for new customers. I shared my screen with groups of strangers and pointed-and-clicked through demo dashboards modeled after hypothetical companies' data sets. *Don't worry*, I would reassure them, riffing on a well-worn script, *this is dummy data*. I asked my parents to join, as if to prove that I had moved away from them to do something useful, and one morning, they did. My mother emailed after the session to offer her feedback. *Keep that perky tone!* she wrote, crushingly.

The tool should have been straightforward. It was, in theory, simple enough to be used by a marketing manager. At least, that's what my coworkers said—a blessing upon modern software. For years, the catchphrase had been *So easy, your mother could use it*, but this had grown uncouth and politically incorrect, to be used only in meetings where women weren't present, of which there were plenty. But our users were endlessly creative in their ability to implement it incorrectly. They activated their own code, only to find that ours was silent, unresponsive. They checked their dashboards, refreshed and restarted their browsers. Then they would email, angrily.

I don't see any data, they wrote. They wanted to know: What was wrong with the software? Were our servers down? Did we know they were paying us thousands, and for nothing? They were convinced that the tool was broken; they were convinced they could not be at fault. These notes were laced with anxiety. Some customers would panic, level accusations, disparage the company on social media. There was a small part of me that relished their frustration: I knew that I would fix it. There were no unsolvable problems. Perhaps there were not even problems, only mistakes.

My job was to reassure them that the software was not broken—to remind them that our software was never broken. Step by step, I would begin to debug their processes. Sometimes this involved looking at a customer's source code or data, where, once inside, I could begin to untangle the errors. This was like working a pin through a snarled necklace: slow, deliberate, prone to backsliding. With quiet satisfaction, I explained to customers exactly where things had gone haywire, and then found ways to take responsibility for their errors. I reassured them that our product was complicated, though it should not have been complicated for them. I conceded that our documentation should have been clearer, even if I had just written that piece of documentation myself. I apologized, over and over, for mistakes that they had made. *Does that make sense?* I'd ask every few minutes, as gently as a tutor, giving them space to shift the blame back to me.

For particularly difficult cases, we took to the telephone. We didn't have desk phones, so I gave out my personal mobile number. In a text-based industry, speaking on the phone was surprisingly intimate. Unless the customer was verbally abusive, I liked doing it. Most understood that customer support wasn't coming from an outsourced call center in the middle of Indiana; it was just coming from me. I would roll a desk chair into the brutally air-conditioned server room, drink tea, and repeat myself until it felt like we had come to an understanding. Sometimes a customer and I opted to video-chat and screen-share, but this felt like too much exposure, too much person-hood. I was always unnerved to sign in to the meeting and see my own face floating above the pixelated head of a stranger, blinking back.

Offline, away from the cold portals of their inboxes and our support ticketing system, customers tended to get more personal. On Solutions, we often spoke about how to "surprise and delight" our users—a customer-service lesson promoted by the online superstore—but sometimes our users were the ones to surprise me. They told me about their workplace conflicts; they talked about their divorces and online dates.

One of the customers told me to look up his blog, which I did immediately, skimming his posts about vacations and strength training, as I gave him instructions over the phone on how to use our data-export API. I clarified how to format request parameters while scrolling through photographs of his ex-wife eating lobster rolls; standing akimbo on various mountains; holding their cat, who had died. A few days later, we struck up a para-professional email correspondence—about my yearning for New York and his foibles with online dating—but I backed off when it grew too intimate. We never met.

Some days, helping men solve problems they had created for themselves, I felt like a piece of software myself, a bot: instead of being an artificial intelligence, I was an intelligent artifice, an empathetic text snippet or a warm voice, giving instructions, listening comfortingly. At the top of every email the men received, my avatar, a photo taken in Brooklyn by a close friend, smiled shyly from behind a curtain of hair.

Twice a week, around six or seven in the evening, contractors for a food-delivery app would walk off the elevator, pushing carts stacked with sturdy tin troughs. The operations manager would line the troughs up on a counter near the kitchen, and as soon as she had peeled back the foil coverings, my coworkers would jump up from their desks and race to be first in line for self-serve. It didn't matter to me that meals in the office weren't a bonding opportunity or a gesture of care, but a business decision—an incentive to stay inside, stay longer, keep grinding. The food was low-carb and delicious, well worth someone else's money, healthier than anything I ever cooked. I was glad to share another meal with my teammates. We sat happily at the lunch tables, shoveling it into our bodies.

One evening, over dinner, the CEO encouraged me to expand my scope: learn how to code, start doing work outside of my job description. "Make it so that they'll have no option but to promote you," he advised. Who was "they," I wondered—wasn't "they" him? He told me he would personally promote me to solutions architect if I could build a networked, two-player game of checkers. When he got back to his desk, he emailed me a PDF of a programming manual that promised to make beginners proficient in JavaScript over the course of a weekend.

Engineers I knew talked about how the world had opened up to them the first time they wrote a functional line of code. The system belonged to them; the computer would do their bidding. They were in control. They could build everything they'd ever imagined. They talked about achieving flow, a sustained state of mental absorption and joyful focus, like a runner's high obtained without having to exercise. I loved that they used this terminology. It sounded so menstrual.

Working in tech without a technical background felt like moving to a foreign country without knowing the language. I didn't mind trying. Programming was tedious, but it wasn't hard. I found some enjoyment in its clarity: it was like math, or copy-editing. There was an order, a clear distinction between right and wrong. When I had edited or vetted manuscripts at the literary agency, I moved primarily on instinct and feeling, with the constant terror that I would ruin someone else's creative work. Code, by contrast, was responsive and uncaring. Like nothing else in my life, when I made a mistake, it let me know immediately.

I spent a weekend dutifully completing the programming exercises while thinking about all the other things I would rather be doing, like reading a novel, or writing postcards to my friends back home, or exploring a new neighborhood on my bike. I was not excited to be in control of the machine. I did not achieve flow. There was nothing I needed or desired from software. There was nothing I wanted to hack or build. I didn't need to outsource another part of my life to an app, and I never played checkers. The part of my brain that took some pleasure in coding also thrived on obsessive-compulsive behavior and perfectionism. It wasn't the part of my brain that I wanted to nurture.

Later, I would recount the challenge to the engineers, who were appalled: networked checkers, they said, wasn't a beginner's activity—the CEO had sent me on a wild-goose chase. But at the time, my lack of interest in learning JavaScript felt like a moral failure. I returned the following Monday and told the CEO I couldn't do it. This seemed, in that environment, like a lesser evil than not wanting to.

•

Around my two-month mark, the solutions manager took me for a walk around the neighborhood. We ambled through a small park well suited to short corporate lunch dates and low-stakes breakups. We passed a strip club, a popular spot for parties during developer conferences, that my coworkers claimed had a superlative lunch buffet. We crossed in front of people eating eighteen-dollar salads; we circumvented people sleeping over steaming grates.

The solutions manager told me he was proud of me, that I had scaled up quickly: I was already able to answer the majority of the questions in the inbox, could hold my own against a botched implementation, was providing excellent support to our customers. The company felt they had made a good investment. As a token of good faith, he said, they were giving me a raise. He looked at me with kind eyes, as if he had given birth to me.

"We're giving you an extra ten thousand dollars," he said, "because we want to keep you."

I abandoned the rent control. I moved out of the Castro and into a one-room apartment on the first floor of a creaky Edwardian in the northern part of the city, above the fog line. I rode in the back of the moving truck with a mattress, two duffels, and my six or seven boxes of belongings: half a mile down Divisadero, half a mile up Haight. It took the movers thirty minutes, door to door—a job so small, so pathetic, that when it came time to pay they insisted on a discount.

The studio was tiny and bright and mine. There were bars on the bay window, but I didn't care—there was a bay window, and it looked out over an old and twisted Australian tea tree. In the bathroom was a narrow shower stall that made me feel like a Damien Hirst cow. A back door led to the basement, through which I could access a shared garden with a redwood tree and a regal, dying palm.

Rent was eighteen hundred dollars a month, about 40 percent of my monthly take-home pay. I didn't expect to stay longer than a year: I would reinvent myself professionally, I figured, and return to New York with a midlevel managerial title and marketable skills. Besides, I had never lived alone before, and now had 275 square feet to myself. It felt like total privacy. The door locked in four places.

The real estate agent who showed me the apartment had asked to meet early in the morning, and forty-eight hours after he handed off the keys, I understood why. The apartment faced the street, and people hung out on the corner, playing guitar, picking fights, and hawking drugs, in stage whispers, to passersby. They squatted against the tea tree and shot up, broke up, brawled, pissed. Some had long, bad trips, screaming about God or for their mothers. Some slouched outside an old movie theater around the block, recently reincarnated as a modern commune catering to the digital-nomad set, petting their dogs and panhandling. A neighbor referred to them as trust-fund babies. "You can tell by their teeth who's had orthodontia," he said, rolling his eyes, as we retrieved our mail from adjacent boxes. I didn't know whether he meant the homeless millennials or the digital nomads, and didn't ask.

At night, when I got home, it felt almost like a different city. There were minimal traces of the ecosystem. San Francisco's micro-neighborhoods were committed to well-worn urban identities: the Castro, a landing strip of innuendo-laden retail descending from a plaza where nudists drank coffee at bistro tables, their genitals stuffed into athletic socks, had been a crash course in a certain style of revisionist nostalgia. But the Haight, with its sky-high catcallers and teenaged purveyors of purple kush, was perhaps most committed of all.

The neighborhood had incubated the sixties counterculture, and nearly fifty years later nobody seemed willing to give that identity up. Visitors from all over the world arrived as if on a pilgrimage, looking for something that may never have existed.

Families wandered the main drag, dipping into head shops and vintage stores, taking photographs in front of murals depicting famous and long-dead musicians. They skirted teenagers lying on the curb outside the free clinic and averted their eyes from the vans parked on the street, hand-roll windows blocked with towels and newspaper.

At sundown, in the doorways of stores selling tie-dye leggings and postcards of acid pioneers, people curled up in second-hand camping gear and atop cardboard boxes, a slightly safer option than sleeping in the park. It was possible that the tourists trawling the commercial strip mistook San Francisco's homelessness epidemic for part of the hippie aesthetic. It was possible that the tourists didn't think about the homelessness epidemic at all.

Weekends, once I ran out of work, were a challenge. Sometimes I met up with coworkers, but mostly I spent time alone. I felt free, invisible, and very lonely. On warm afternoons, I went to Golden Gate Park and lay in the grass listening to dance music, fantasizing about going out dancing. People threw tennis balls to their dogs in corridors of light, and I felt envious. I watched groups of fitness enthusiasts bobbing up and down and wondered if I was the sort of person who could make friends doing squats.

The city's green spaces overflowed with heterosexual couples jogging in tandem and cycling next to each other on bikes with matching panniers. It was impossible to walk through a park without seeing a man in a heather-gray T-shirt running suicides or doing obliques. There was, on public display, an unfathomable level of wholesomeness.

I took long, solo bike rides. I took my phone out to dinner.

I walked the curve of Lands End, listening to Arthur Russell and feeling sorry for myself. I walked to an independent movie theater in Japantown, to see a close friend from college in her first feature. Her giant lips parted onscreen; I sipped hard on a cup of seltzer and held back tears.

I eavesdropped on conversations in parks and restaurants, listening eagerly to strangers my age gossip about other strangers. I wrote long, detailed descriptions of nothing, and sent them by email to friends. I went to concerts alone and attempted to make deep and prolonged eye contact with the musicians. I brought magazines to bars and sat by dingy electric fireplaces, hoping and not-hoping that someone would talk to me. No one ever did.

My single coworkers were all on multiple dating apps, and encouraged me to follow suit. But I found myself newly cautious, leery of giving away too much intimate data. God Mode had made me paranoid. It wasn't the act of data collection itself, to which I was already resigned. What gave me pause was the people who might see it on the other end—people like me. I never knew with whom I was sharing my information.

Instead of posting a photograph of my own face to the app, I uploaded a collage of a Slovenian philosopher responsible for reintroducing Marxism to a certain subset of my generation—mostly men whose living rooms held extensive vinyl collections and proud little libraries packed with the critical theory and art history books they'd half read in college—superimposed onto an orange astronaut suit. I'd made the collage years ago, probably to signal to a crush that I was both funny and serious, the sort of person a man could talk at for hours about topological networks of bioracism or the necropolitics of recycling.

I spent hours in bed, drinking coffee and thumbing at my phone. I made plans with two separate men who seemed boring and benign, if well versed in social theory, before deciding I couldn't go through with it: What kind of sociopath, I wondered, would be drawn to my profile? I stopped replying and deleted the app.

A few days later, I was alarmed to see that one of the men had messaged me on the social network everyone hated. I'd never given him my full name, and was careful about minimizing my digital footprint. I tried to reverse engineer how he'd identified me, and couldn't.

It hadn't been hard to find me, the man claimed. I would waste hours of my life trying to figure out how.

A friend from high school emailed to introduce me to an engineer he knew, and the engineer and I agreed to meet for drinks. It wasn't clear whether we were being set up for a date, or to network; it wasn't clear there was so much of a difference. I wore a dress, just in case. Keyhole over my cleavage. Bike shorts underneath.

The engineer was very handsome and stiltedly sweet, the sort of man who probably hung out on the website for people who called themselves creatives. He worked at a large social media company, and was an early enough employee that he spoke of it with a sense of ownership. We offered each other oral histories of our own résumés while eating tonkatsu off biodegradable plates.

After busing our own table, the engineer suggested we repair to a tiny cocktail bar in the Tenderloin. As we walked past an open-air drug market, I wondered if we would run into the CTO. I wondered if he would be disappointed to see me hanging out with another software developer, instead of all the countercultural friends I had bragged about over lunch.

The bar had textured wallpaper and a scrawny bouncer.

Photographs were forbidden, which meant the place was designed to be leaked on social media, a coup of guerrilla marketing. Everyone inside the bar looked very proud of themselves.

"There's no menu, so you can't just order, you know, a martini," the engineer told me, as if I would ever. "You tell the bartender three adjectives, and he'll customize a drink for you accordingly. I've been thinking about my adjectives all day." What was it like to be fun, I wondered—what was it like to feel you'd earned this?

I tried to game the system by asking for something smoky, salty, and angry, crossing my fingers for mescal; it worked. We leaned against a wall and sipped. The engineer told me about his loft in the Mission, his specialty bikes, his habitual weeknight camping trips. We talked about digital SLRs and books. He seemed like someone who would have opinions about fonts.

When the engineer went to the bathroom, I looked up his account on the photo-sharing app and scrolled through: fog at Lands End, fog on Muir Beach, crashing waves, copper hills. The Golden Gate Bridge at daybreak, at sunset, at night. Half the photographs featured either his bicycle or a strip of empty road. They were, I had to admit, very high resolution.

It seemed stressful to me, cultivating a public image, or a personal aesthetic—like the sort of mind-set that could lead a person to worry during sex about whether the lighting was sufficiently cinematic. I knew I didn't fit into the engineer's meticulously curated life. I knew we'd never hang out again, though I also knew that I would try. Even so, I biked home that night feeling like something, however small, had been lifted.

The CEO's girlfriend, it turned out, also needed friends. Female friends, he clarified. *Go on a girl date*, he wrote, introducing us over email. All I knew about his girlfriend was that she was also a software engineer, at a computer-animation studio famous for its high-end children's entertainment; that they lived in the same building—their apartments separated by a floor, an intentional arrangement that I thought was genius—and, of course, that he loved her.

We met at a wine bar around the corner from the analytics startup and settled onto white leather ottomans near the door. The bar looked like a vestige of the first tech boom, all microsuede and chrome, recessed lighting: a nineties vision board. Lounge music invaded the space. Part of the bar was cordoned off for a company event hosted by a venture firm. Men in Japanese denim, white dress shirts, and name tags gesticulated at one another, gazing past each other's shoulders, looking for better people to network with. I was happy just to leave the office.

The CEO's girlfriend was poised, articulate, sincere, even-keeled. She had shampoo-commercial hair and wore a slim, understated blazer. She described her work as interesting and fun. The products she helped build made people happy, she said. It all sounded so uncomplicated.

As we swapped safe observations about being women in tech, I tried to imagine a life in which we became close. While it was easy to picture her visiting me in the hospital if I ever had a terminal illness, I had a harder time envisioning us getting stoned and watercoloring, or going to an experimental dance performance. What were we going to do, talk about sex? Talk about sexism?

I tried to imagine a life in which I was simply her and the CEO's third wheel. We could sit on the sidelines of the basketball court in Potrero Hill and watch him play pickup. She could teach me how to blow out my hair, and not just in the front. I pictured us going on vacations together, the three of us drinking seltzer and discussing functional programming. Perhaps I, too, could become an executive if I hung out with present and future executives. I would have access to the inside track. We could go on weekend getaways to Sonoma, rent entire houses on the home-sharing platform and stand around marble kitchen islands sipping biodynamic wines and sharing our business ideas. This was as difficult to picture as the two of us getting sweaty at a basement show, or exchanging stoner insights about whether the past was a place.

When the CEO's girlfriend inquired about my job, I deflected. Work was a default topic of conversation, and all-encompassing for me, but I wasn't sure how much she would really want to know, or how much she knew already. I wasn't sure whether she would relay anything I said back to her boyfriend. The possibility gave the evening the tenor of an unofficial performance review—though the possibility that she might say nothing was worse.

The CEO was with us without being with us, and this prevented me both from revealing myself and from seeing her as an independent human. I felt ashamed by my inability to see her fully. I did not like that my primary frame for her was as someone's girlfriend, a sidekick, an appendage, but I couldn't transcend my workplace anxieties. Maybe mutual desire for friends wasn't enough for a friendship. Maybe we just didn't have that much in common.

We drank a glass of wine each, taking small, slow sips. We discussed books we were reading or had purchased with the intent to open, as soon as we had the time. We agreed, liars both, that we would attend a second-run theater production together. We smiled half-apologetically into the conversational silence as we rolled the wine around in our mouths, as if we were drinking something more sophisticated than the house white. Eventually, we finished our drinks, and with a seamless, unspoken intimacy, both declined the waiter's offer of a second.

In midsummer, news broke that a National Security Agency contractor had leaked classified information about the U.S. government's enormous, tentacled surveillance programs. At lunch, my coworkers and I ignored the media apps clogging our phones with push notifications about the story, and debated where to grab takeout: the food court of the mall down the block, or the Mexican place? We returned with passable Thai food and high-saline ramen, and sat down at the large communal tables, where we talked about podcasts and prestige television, bad dates and upcoming vacations. Then we went back to our desks and continued building, selling, supporting, and marketing our software.

Among the whistleblower's revelations was that the NSA was reading private citizens' personal communications: emails and texts, direct messages on social-networking platforms. It was harvesting contact lists and creating communication maps, tracking where and when and with whom Americans were congregating. The NSA was crawling through people's internet activity without their knowledge or consent. It did so by gathering cookies, which allowed user behavior to be mapped and tied together across the web. Cookies were something that I knew more than a little bit about: they were a critical technology for the data-analytics software.

To obtain some of this information, the NSA had turned to the cloud. The idea of the cloud, its implied transparency and ephemerality, concealed the physical reality: the cloud was just a network of hardware, storing data indefinitely. All hardware could be hacked. The servers of global technology companies had been penetrated and pillaged by the government. Some said the technology companies had collaborated wittingly, by creating back doors. Others defended their innocence. It was hard to know with whom to sympathize, or whom to fear.

The part of the story that captured my attention was a minor detail, practically a sidebar. It was revealed that lower-level employees at the NSA, including contractors, had access to the same databases and queries as their high-level superiors. Agents spied on their family members and love interests, nemeses and friends. It was, by all accounts, a nightmare scenario. But it wasn't that hard to imagine.

At the analytics startup, we never once talked about the whistleblower, not even during happy hour. In general, we rarely discussed the news, and we certainly weren't about to start with this story. We didn't think of ourselves as participating in the surveillance economy. We weren't thinking about our role in facilitating and normalizing the creation of unregulated, privately held databases on human behavior. We were just allowing product managers to run better A/B tests. We were just helping developers make better apps. It was all so simple: people loved our product and leveraged it to improve their own products, so that people would love them, too. There was nothing nefarious about it. Besides, if we didn't do it, someone else would. We were far from the only third-party analytics tool on the market.

The sole moral quandary in our space that we acknowledged outright was the question of whether or not to sell data to advertisers. This was something we did not do, and we were righteous about it. We were just a neutral platform, a conduit.

If anyone raised concerns about the information our users were collecting, or the potential for abuse of our product, the solutions manager would try to bring us back to earth by reminding us that we weren't data brokers. We did not build cross-platform profiles. We didn't involve third parties. Users might not know they were being tracked, but that was between them and our customer companies.

"Don't forget, we're on the right side of things," the solutions manager would say, smiling. "We're the good guys."

We were swamped with work, inundated with new customers. Every team needed to hire. Our referral bonus, a new-employee dowry, increased from five thousand dollars per hire to eight. Noah began pulling in a substantial secondary income in referral bonuses, dispatching his younger brothers and parents to help the recruitment effort.

The CEO was picky about hiring: the first hundred employees of the company set the tone for its future, he said. Culture trickled down. It was critical that we be careful about determining its course. This bolstered our sense of self-importance and gratitude for our employment: we were the chosen, an elite few. But it also meant that scaling up was challenging.

I interviewed dozens of candidates for the Solutions team.

How would you describe the internet to a medieval farmer? I asked prospective support engineers, as authoritatively as possible. What's the hardest thing you've ever done?

Almost none of them made it past the founders, who began to get annoyed—I was wasting their time. "Don't hire anyone worse than you," the CEO instructed. He meant this as a compliment.

The CEO and solutions manager agreed we needed more women on Support, but they didn't hire any. Instead, we built out a small cadre of overqualified millennial men fleeing law, finance, education, and dorm-room entrepreneurship. One was a former private equity analyst, fresh from New York, who called me "honey" and dressed in adolescent defiance of Wall Street: combat boots, skinny jeans, and fluffy, oversized sweaters. Another had taught math in Boston's public school system—the startup grind, he said, felt like a vacation by comparison. A third had recently received his Ph.D. in computational biology from an Ivy League university, and referred to himself as "doctor." It was only sort of a joke. With the exception of the doctor, they were all, once again, younger than I was.

The boys were more technical than I had been when I started—better than me—which gave me a complex. Still, we developed an easy rapport. They admired my seniority and complimented my emotional intelligence. They corrected my scripts; I corrected their grammar. They were competitive, and constantly in pursuit of the CEO's acknowledgment and respect. I felt responsible for them, protective.

When some of the support engineers began to exhibit signs of burnout, I suggested to the CEO that complimenting their work might go a long way. They could use the ego boost, I said. Some positive reinforcement couldn't hurt productivity, besides—maybe we'd even see it reflected in their individual success metrics, which I presented to the company during Tuesday meetings. I hated the success metrics, but I liked being the one who monitored them.

The CEO and I didn't always speak each other's language. I was interested in talking about empathy, a buzzword used to the point of pure abstraction, and teaching the support engineers how to properly use punctuation. He was interested in running complex data analysis on our team's performance and holding the boys accountable to numbers. I talked about compassionate analytics. He talked about optimizing. I wanted a team of tender hearts. He wanted a team of machines.

"Why would I thank you for doing your job well?" the CEO asked, frowning. "That's what I'm paying you for."

It didn't take long to see that in Silicon Valley, non-engineers were pressed to prove their value. Hiring the first nontechnical employee was always the end of an era. We bloated payroll; we diluted lunchtime conversation; we created process and bureaucracy; we put in requests for yoga classes and Human Resources. We tended to contribute positively, however, to diversity metrics.

The hierarchy was pervasive at the analytics startup, ingrained in the CEO's dismissal of marketing and insistence that a good product would sell itself. It was reflected in our salaries and equity allotment. Despite evidence that emotional intelligence, unlike programming languages or agile development, could not be taught—there was a reason compassion was a tall hurdle for AI—soft skills were undervalued.

Our operations manager, a public defender before she immigrated to the United States, ran payroll, planned events, pinch-hit as a technical recruiter, worked on the interior design, assisted the CEO, and served as our ad hoc Human Resources department. She chatted in Spanish with the facilities crew and prepared materials for board meetings. She put up with complaints about the snack selection, and took shit for putting baby wipes in the men's bathroom. The founders had hired her, she once told me, because they knew she would get things done, and the founders had been right: she quietly ran the show. I didn't know why this skill set should be any less valued, culturally or monetarily, than the ability to write a Rails app.

Still, I was susceptible to the mythos. I looked for technical self-starters. I prioritized the programming-curious. He just taught himself to code over the summer, I heard myself say of a job candidate one afternoon. It floated out of my mouth with the awe of someone relaying a miracle.

Management arranged for a team-building exercise, scheduled for a weeknight evening. We pregamed at the office lunch tables, drinking with the lights low and the music up. The solutions manager gamely pounded root beers. The Engineering team's Betta fish throbbed in its murky aquarium.

We walked en masse to a tiny event space at the mouth of the Stockton Tunnel. Two energetic blonds, a man and a woman, gave us colorful branded sweatbands. The blonds were attractive and athletic, strong limbs wrapped in spandex leggings and tiny shorts, and we were their foils: an army of soft bellies and stiff necks, hands tight with the threat of carpal tunnel. Noah did a double-take: one of the blonds was a friend of his from high school. The situation would have mortified me, but they embraced, laughing, the picture of breezy Californian male friendship.

The event space warmed up as people got drunk and bounced around the room, taking selfies with the CTO and fist-bumping the cofounders without irony. We played carnival games, tossed miniature basketballs against the rims of miniature hoops. We clustered by the bar and had another round, two.

Eventually, we were dispatched on a scavenger hunt across the city. We poured out of the building and into the street, spreading across rush-hour San Francisco, seeking landmarks. We made human pyramids in the center of Union Square, snapped each other's sweatbands, photographed ourselves mid-jump on the steps of an old, regal bank. We barreled past tourists and harassed taxicab drivers, pissed off doormen and stumbled into homeless people.

We were our own worst representatives, tearing through the city, shouting apologies over our shoulders. We were sweaty, competitive—even happy, maybe happy.

One morning, a meeting was dropped mysteriously onto our calendars. The last time this happened, we were given forms that asked us to rate various values on a scale of 1 to 5: our desire to lead a team; the importance of work-life balance. I gave both things a 4 and was told I didn't want them enough.

At the designated time, we shuffled into a conference room, shrugging. The conference room had a million-dollar view of downtown San Francisco, but we kept the shades down. Across the street, a bucket drummer banged out an irregular heartbeat.

We sat in a row, backs to the window, laptops open. I looked around the room and felt a wave of affection for these men, this small group of misfits who were the only people who understood the backbone to my new life. On the other side of the table, the solutions manager paced back and forth, but he was smiling. He asked us to write down the names of the five smartest people we knew, and my coworkers dutifully obliged.

Smart in exactly what way, I wondered, capping and uncapping my pen. I was not accustomed to stack-ranking my friends by intelligence. I wrote five names down: a sculptor, a writer, a physicist, two graduate students. I looked at the list and thought about how much I missed them, how bad I'd been at returning phone calls and emails. I wondered how I'd stopped making time for the things and people I held dear. I felt blood rush to my cheeks.

"Okay," the solutions manager said. "Now tell me, why don't they work here?"

Why didn't my smartest friends work there? It was hard to confront, but not because it was complicated.

My friends wouldn't have found the work fulfilling or meaningful. They weren't interested in other businesses' business metrics. They didn't care for tech and, for the most part, they weren't motivated by money, not yet. Those who were motivated by money could make more of it doing something else: finance, medicine, law, consulting. They already did.

Startup culture was not for them. They would have taken one look at the company website and balked. A slideshow blinked across the jobs page: group photos in which we all wore our data-driven T-shirts; group photos in which we sat on each other's shoulders, making faces. Photos of the CEO and my coworkers voluntarily participating in a fear-based endurance event near Tahoe, a massive obstacle course where they swam through dumpsters of ice water and plowed across muddy fields while being administered electric shocks by former Division II athletes. Photos of me, modeling the company T-shirt, thick-necked and grinning.

My friends were hardworking and committed, but their vocations were poorly compensated, and against that rubric their life choices were wholly unimpressive. They were the sort of people some tech workers looked down on for not contributing meaningfully to the economy, though the derision cut both ways—if anyone our age had ever introduced himself as an entrepreneur, my friends would have laughed themselves into fits of smug superiority.

In any case, my friends' world was sensuous, emotional, complex. It was theoretical and expressive. It could, at times, be chaotic. This was not the world that analytics software facilitated. It was a world I wasn't sure I could still call mine.

If, in New York, I had never considered that there were people behind the internet, in San Francisco it was impossible to forget. Bubbly startup logos glowed from the tops of warehouses and office towers, and adorned the hats and vests and cycling kits of commuters downtown.

The city was dotted with reminders that the English language was being disrupted. The stretch of highway that swept Silicon Valley, from San Francisco down to San Jose—where the money really started to tumble; where billboard space cost the most—was flanked with advertisements pitching software products to software developers in a language that only somewhat resembled modern speech. The ads transcended all context and grammatical structure. WE FIXED DINNER (meal delivery). HOW TOMORROW WORKS (file storage). ASK YOUR DEVELOPER (cloud-based communications). They looked futuristic and strange alongside the more traditional advertisements, although the older industries were starting to better understand their new target market. A financial-services company—one that had been around for more than a century, a provider of life insurance, investment management, and, in the 1980s, bald-faced fraud—stuck to the conventions of grammar, but held a mirror to an audience that perhaps wouldn't want to recognize itself. That ad read DONATE TO A WORTHY CAUSE: YOUR RETIREMENT.

Descending the train station escalator one evening, I noticed an ad covering the platform below. The product was a password-storage app—identity as a service—but the company wasn't advertising to users; they were advertising their job openings. They were advertising to me.

The ad featured five people standing in V-formation with their arms crossed. They were all wearing identical blue hoodies. They were also wearing identical rubber unicorn masks. I walked off the escalator and onto one of their heads. The copy read BUILT BY HUMANS, USED BY UNICORNS.

What was anyone ever talking about? People said things like "co-execute" and "upleveling"; they used "ask" and "attach" and "fail" as nouns. They joked about "adulting." They substituted viral memes for social currency. They deployed internet slang as if it constituted a vocabulary—as if acronyms weren't already standing in for other words. "You know that animated GIF of the stick figure?" a coworker in his early twenties asked, to describe his emotional state. I did not. "Lol," he said, not laughing. Ha ha, I said. Not laughing.

None of the startups in the ecosystem were named for posterity, and certainly not for history. Naming standards were dictated by URL availability, forcing new companies to get creative. Somewhere, a branding studio was raking it in convincing startup founders to sound illiterate. Entrepreneurs formed LLCs under fabricated portmanteaus, or nouns with the vowels removed. I resigned myself to a future where, if I got lucky, my grandchildren's college tuition would be thanks to some company that sounded like accidental metathesis, or a Freudian slip.

Sometimes it felt like everyone was speaking a different language—or the same language with radically different rules. There was no common lexicon. Instead, people used a sort of nonlanguage, which was neither beautiful nor especially efficient: a mash-up of business-speak with athletic and wartime metaphors, inflated with self-importance. Calls to action; front lines and trenches; blitzscaling. Companies didn't fail, they died. We didn't compete, we went to war.

"We are making products," the CEO said, building us up at a Tuesday team meeting, "that can push the fold of mankind."

On a chilly morning in late summer, the fog still lingering, we took a field trip to see our own, newly unveiled highway billboards. Everyone got to work early. The operations manager ordered fresh-squeezed orange juice and pastries, cups of yogurt parfait with granola strata. A bottle of champagne sat on the table, unopened.

I was proud of our communications director, and nervous for her. It was unclear what metrics could be associated with a highway billboard. The CEO already didn't believe in marketing. He believed in networks. Word of mouth. He believed in making something so useful, so necessary, so well designed that it insinuated itself into people's lives without external pressures. Billboards were wildly expensive. It would be difficult, if not impossible, to prove the return on investment.

We walked down into SoMa in a pack, hands in our pockets.

We took a group photograph in front of one of our ads, arms around one another, smiling and proud. I forwarded the photo to my parents in New York, promising, guiltily, that I would call home soon.

Noah took me under his wing. Meeting his friends was like swinging open the gate to a side of the Bay Area I thought had been pushed out. Here were chefs and social workers, academics and musicians, dancers and poets. Few were employed full-time. They practiced radical honesty and believed in nonreligious spiritual orientation. They spoke in the language of encounter groups. They sat in each other's laps and snuggled in public. They owned costume boxes. It was not unusual, at parties, to walk into a bedroom and find someone administering Reiki.

Everyone was sorting out a way to live. Some of the women instituted systems of gender reparations with their male partners. Staunch atheists bought tarot decks and fretted over how best to infuse them with powerful energy; they discussed rising signs and compared astrological birth charts. They went to outposts in Mendocino to supervise each other through sustained, high-dose LSD trips, intended to reveal their inner children to their adult selves.

They journaled, and discussed their journaling. They went on retreats to technology-liberation summer camps, where they locked up their smartphones and traded their legal names 'for pseudonyms invoking animals, berries, meteorological phenomena. They traveled to cliffside silent-meditation plantations, and wandered around for days afterward, inarticulate and asocial. Some spread the word about a famous leadership and self-help program. When I looked it up, I discovered that it was widely regarded as a cult.

It seemed like half of the new-school old-schoolers spent the bulk of their spare time on overstuffed secondhand couches, drinking tea and processing. Processing was a daily routine, a group activity. People consulted one another on their romantic entanglements, their financial problems, their hemorrhoids. Everyone was always checking in.

I struggled to assimilate. I tried ecstatic dance, but spent most of the time on the sidelines, adjusting my socks. I participated in massage chains, fully clothed. I asked a graphically untalented animal-rights activist to paint my face at a party, and danced on the edges, trying to force my mind out of my body. I attended a spa-themed party at a communal house and wandered the grounds in a robe, avoiding the hot tub—a sous vide bath of genitalia.

Processing as a hobby made me feel an affinity for the cool, impersonal bullshit of business culture. Radical honesty often looked to me like a collapse of the barrier between subjectivity and objectivity. It could look like cruelty. But it also seemed to work.

I did not want to judge them. I admired their collectivity, which seemed to me wholesome and intimate. The trust among friends was familial, openhearted, optimistic. There was true community. The future was blurred and the present was unstable. Life was characterized, to varying degrees, by persistent precariousness. Everyone was doing what they could to keep a toehold on the city, to keep a part of the culture sacrosanct; to build what they believed would be a better world.

At a birthday party north of the Panhandle, Noah's roommate, Ian, sat down beside me and struck up a conversation. I felt, all of a sudden, very beautiful and interesting. Never in my life had I pulled a man across a crowded room. Later, I would learn that this was just Ian's approach to social gatherings: as a software engineer who hung out almost exclusively with people who had majored in the humanities, he was sensitive to outsiders, predisposed to seek out and engage the person who looked most bored at a party. I had been sitting alone on the couch, not talking to anyone, trying to keep my feet from tapping to the tropical house playing out of someone's phone, and staring at the bookcase: programming manuals, books about ethical polyamory. His was an easy kindness.

Ian was soft-spoken and whistled, lightly, when he pronounced the letter S. He had static-electricity hair and a sweet, narrow smile. He asked questions and then asked follow-up questions, a novelty. It took a while for me to steer the conversation over to him. What do you do, I asked, like the East Coast careerist I was. He worked in robotics, he said, but didn't feel like talking about it at a party. A man who worked in tech who didn't want to talk about tech: very endearing.

Our trajectories had been asymptotic, we discovered. Ian and I had friends in common—mostly editors and writers in Brooklyn, whom he knew from college. His band had played a show in the basement of my sophomore dorm. I had even been in his apartment, I remembered, on a detour during a particularly boozy Solutions team outing. He'd been home that night, he said, cooking dinner in the back. The more we compared notes, the stranger it seemed that we had not yet met. I wanted to put my hands in his hair.

We wandered into the kitchen together, in pursuit of fresh beverages. A cluster of people sat on the linoleum, drinking wine out of jam jars. "What is your most or least favorite trait inherited from your parents?" one of them was asking, with great solemnity. A man wearing a fleece onesie with attached slippers leaned forward, placing his chin in his palms. "Resilience," he said. Everyone nodded. "And do you feel like they see that in you?" someone else inquired.

Nightmare, I thought. I eyed the back door. The prospect of engaging in therapeutic maieutics with a group of strangers was stressful. I could not fathom interrogating my relationship with my parents as a form of socializing. I felt uptight, conservative, repressed, corporate by comparison—but I also felt okay with that. Ian grabbed two cans of beer and nodded toward the hall.

Back in the living room, people were beginning to mobilize for karaoke: wetting down the hookah charcoal, collecting empties, wrapping road-beers in handkerchiefs and recycled paper. Ian and I continued talking as the party paraded toward Japantown. I felt calm around him, at home. Winding through Alamo Square Park, he gently took my hand and put it in his jacket pocket, holding it there as we walked.

Noah and Ian lived on the second floor of a former fire station in the Mission, on a block-long street wedged between two main drags that represented, in near-Dickensian fashion, the city's socioeconomic cleft. In one direction was a chaotic plaza at Mission and Sixteenth—a convocation of commuters, rose vendors, homeless people, addicts, prostitutes, pigeons, and soft-eyed drunks—that opened onto a bustling avenue of doughnut shops, Mexican bakeries, fish markets, Pentecostal churches, dollar stores, holes-in-the-wall stuffed with boxes of cleats, mobile grills exhaling sausage and onion, smoke shops, unfussy restaurants, and hair salons with hand-painted signage. In the other direction was Valencia Street, a living diorama of late-stage gentrification: third-wave-coffee shops selling paleo lattes, juice bars hawking turmeric shots, waifish Australians clutching branded paper bags from spartan boutiques.

The apartment was cozy and welcoming, full of strange artifacts: an upright piano with the hammers exposed, a headless mannequin covered in hand-drawn hieroglyphs. In the bathroom, a small line of half-melted havdalah candles lined the edge of the tub. The third roommate was a medical resident who kept impossible hours, appearing only occasionally to make generous pots of oatmeal or host men's circles in the living room. It seemed like the sort of place where the roommates would share towels, laying claim to whichever smelled least like mildew, and it was. I loved being there.

That fall, Noah was experimenting with larger-format communal living and had sublet his room to start a collective in Berkeley. During our lunch breaks, he spoke with gravity about chore charts, synchronized calendars, vegetable beds, house meetings. His bedroom was a toolshed, converted illegally, outside of which his younger brother cultivated mushrooms. I was relieved not to worry about running into him in the Mission apartment, one or both of us pattering around half-naked, collapsing an already eroded barrier between work and life.

Ian didn't own a bed frame or a duvet cover, and the bedroom walls were painted an eye-popping primary blue—but he was color-blind, and I liked sleeping low to the ground. Small collections of psychologically revealing objects dotted the room: acorn boughs, cassette tapes, postcards, a toolbox full of electronic components. In the mornings, we would lie in bed and watch the light move across the wall, and I would feel, below the level of the desk and the night table and the bookcase, underwater. At the last possible minute, we would throw on clothes and helmets, hoist our bikes down the stairs, and part ways at the building's front gate, wheeling carefully around pools of broken glass.

Ian worked at a small robotics studio that operated out of a large warehouse in Potrero Hill. The studio was full of machine tools, fabrication experiments, props, and soundstages. Two employees ran a small brewing operation from a side room. In the main space were human-sized robotic arms, typically used on assembly lines, which Ian and a small team programmed to do camerawork for films and commercials. The films were beautiful, intimate and sweeping at once.

Earlier that year, the studio had been acquired by the search-engine giant. One of the founders had been sent a set of three-hundred-thousand-dollar speakers as a welcome gift; when a pallet of electric skateboards arrived at the studio, Ian and his coworkers knew the deal had closed. The acquisition was part of a multibillion-dollar shopping spree, in service of a new robotics division named after an android from an eighties sci-fi film. The newly acquired engineers and inventors, hundreds of them, would be tasked with building the autonomous, streamlined, physical future.

For some, getting acquired by the search-engine giant was a Silicon Valley endgame—a fantasy realized. Ian felt fortunate, but he was ambivalent about the transition. There was a reason he had never sought employment at any of the larger tech conglomerates, a reason he preferred the smaller scale. He had relished being part of an organization where engineers were outnumbered by artists, architects, designers, and filmmakers.

Still, he seemed cautiously excited. The search-engine giant had acquired an impressive spectrum of robotics companies. "I feel like we have a chance to participate in a project that could really leave its mark on the field," he said one evening, as we cooked dinner in my kitchen. "It feels like we're going to have a seat at the table for something really big."

How big? I wanted to know. There were public rumors about what the robotics suite was working on, but Ian was forbidden from speaking about their projects. He refused to confirm my guesses. Was he working on the autonomous cars? I had so many questions. Was it the search-and-rescue robots? The delivery drones? Was there a space shuttle? How soon would we see humanoids? How scared should the rest of us be?

"Everyone always asks me that," he said, frowning. "Not scared. Really." More, I said—say more. In a city where bars and coffee shops and parties were trade-secret word clouds, this was a regionally specific litmus test. But even when we were blindingly drunk, or sliding around the Hirst shower, Ian kept company secrets. It was easy to trust him.

In late fall, Ian brought me to a party at the offices of a clandestine hardware startup operating out of an ivy-clad brick warehouse in Berkeley. Drones buzzed over a crowd of young professionals wearing sensible footwear and fleece vests. A child scuttled underfoot. I felt overdressed in a publishing-era silk blouse.

After making the rounds, Ian disappeared with a coworker to investigate a prototype line of self-assembling modular furniture, leaving me in a circle with a half dozen other roboticists. I sipped on a beer and waited for someone to notice me. Instead, the men discussed work projects using secret code names. They discussed their graduate research. One had spent seven years trying to teach robots to tie different kinds of knots, like Boy Scouts. I asked if he was studying robotics at one of the universities in the Bay Area. No, he said, looking me up and down—he was a professor.

Talk turned to self-driving cars. One of the engineers mentioned a recent Take Your Child to Work Day, where the autonomous-car unit had asked visiting children to jump and dance and roll around in front of the sensors. The technology was world-class, but it still needed to train on nonadults. It was an incredibly exciting moment for transportation, he said: the hurdles they faced weren't technical, but cultural. The biggest obstacle was public opinion.

How plausible were autonomous cars, really, I asked loudly. I had finished my beer and I was bored. I wanted attention, some acknowledgment. I wanted to make sure everyone knew I wasn't just some engineer's girlfriend who stood around at parties waiting for him to finish geeking out—though of course that's exactly what I was doing.

I was skeptical, I told the men. The media hype seemed more than overblown: self-driving cars were part of a future vision that seemed not just unlikely, but beyond fantasy. Hadn't we just established that the cars didn't even know how to identify children? The group turned toward me. The scout-leader professor looked amused.

"What did you say you do?" one of the men asked. I explained that I worked at a mobile analytics company, hoping they would assume I was an engineer. "Ah," he said generously, "and what do you do there?" Customer support, I said. The men glanced at each other. "Don't worry about it," the professor said. He turned back to the others.

fed him. We were fascinated by his psychology. We wanted to figure him out.

"If I had to guess," a sales engineer said over drinks one evening, "he had a childhood where people were not particularly nice to him. I wouldn't have been nice to him. But because he never felt included, he's really distrusting of people's motivations, and really defensive of whatever authority he's able to gain."

"I don't think he likes seeing people suffer," an account manager said, "but he knows producing suffering in people is productive."

"Look up sick systems," said Noah. "Look up trauma bonding. It's the culty thing: keep people busy until they forget about the parts of their life they left behind."

We all knew that the CEO had his own demons. He had to be full of pain and fear like anyone else. He threw around the word "paranoid," but of course he was at least a little bit paranoid—how could he not be? He probably wondered, every day, when the other shoe was going to drop; when everything he touched would stop turning to gold.

I was reluctant to entertain the idea that the CEO was egomaniacal or vindictive. I liked him. There was something familiar about him that was comforting. He reminded me of my high school classmates from a math-and-science magnet in Manhattan: boys who were mathematically brilliant and slightly socially awkward, encouraged but underestimated, and, in almost every case, subject to an unbelievable amount of pressure. I liked that he had an enthusiasm for technology, understanding how things worked. It wasn't about the money for him, I was sure. It was about making something people valued, solving a new problem, getting it right. I assumed he had his reasons, something to prove. An unknown email address was bcc'd on all our support tickets; the solutions manager intimated that it belonged to the CEO's mother.

In any case, I had always appreciated people whose praise and affection were hard-won. I assumed the CEO's reticence indicated he meant what he said. I assumed everyone was doing the best that they could. I wasn't, at the time, thinking about power, manipulation, or control.

I felt very protective of the CEO—or, at least, of my idea of him. For a long time, I would harbor a free-floating sympathy for people I imagined hadn't had the opportunity to experience their youth the way I had. He never had space to fuck up. He'd been under pressure—and a certain degree of surveillance—from venture capitalists and journalists and industry peers since he was twenty. At the age when I was getting drunk with friends on bottles of three-dollar merlot and stumbling into concerts, splitting clove cigarettes and going to slam-poetry open mics, he was worrying about headcount, reading up on unit economics. I was exploring my sexuality; he was comparing health insurance providers and running security audits. Now, at twenty-five, he was responsible for other adults' livelihoods. Some of my co-workers had families, even if they tried not to talk too much about their children in the office. Surely, he felt that weight.

It would take me a while to realize how rarefied the CEO's world was. He was surrounded by people who were crushing it, and people who had chosen him. Kingmakers. People who did not like to admit defeat. The CEO's community was the business community, and it would take care of him. He wasn't in peril. Even if the company was a failure, he could easily fundraise for a new one, or, in the worst-case scenario, become a VC. Unlike the rest of us, he could never backslide.

When the CEO's family came to visit, he toured them through the office quickly. Your parents must be really proud of you, I said, as he came back to our cluster to answer emails. I knew that sentimentality was not his preferred emotional register. I knew I was being too tender, but I couldn't help it—I felt a deep compassion toward him. *I* was proud of him—though I kept that to myself.

The CEO only shrugged. "Maybe," he said.

Noah had been with the startup for a year, and was preparing for his annual review. In advance of the meeting, he sent me his self-assessment and a memo he had written, asking for feedback. As an early, well-respected employee, Noah was often the recipient of grievances and concerns from teammates and customers. In the memo, these came to a head: he agitated for changes to the product and changes in the company culture.

He also agitated for himself: for a title change, more autonomy, a raise, and an increase in stock options. He wanted equity commensurate with his contributions, about 1 percent of the company. Noah presented the data: the number of hires he'd referred, the accounts he—and his referrals—had acquired and nurtured, the amount of money he calculated he had generated for the company, both directly and indirectly. He wanted to become a product manager, to run his own team, and to override the CEO on any related decisions. He framed it as an ultimatum.

Offering the chief executive an ultimatum was unprofessional, crazy, even for one of the best employees at the company. On the other hand, it was a company of twentysomethings run by twentysomethings. The CEO had never had a full-time job; he had only ever held a summer internship. The work environment was one where offering an ultimatum seemed within the bounds of acceptable behavior. It was an incredibly strange place to learn how to be a professional.

The memo was passionate; it radiated frustration. I read through it twice. Then I wrote back to Noah and told him what I believed to be true: it was risky, but it wasn't unreasonable. I hoped they would give him whatever he wanted.

A few days later, en route to work, I received a text message from Noah, telling me he had been fired. When I got to the office, the cluster felt like a funeral home. "They didn't even try to negotiate with him," a sales engineer said in disbelief. "Not a single negotiation. They just let go of one of our best people, all because nobody here has any management experience."

"I don't know," the account manager said, buttering his toast. "You know how, when you want to break up with someone, you twist and turn until they break up with you?" I did not. I thought about how I had signed off on Noah's memo and felt nauseous with guilt.

Previous firings had catalyzed company-wide emails with what was probably an inappropriate level of detail about why the team member had been let go. In lieu of an email, the early members of the Solutions team were corralled into an unscheduled meeting with the CEO. None of us should have been privy to someone else's personnel issue, but we didn't have a Human Resources department. Besides, we wanted to know. We all wondered whether one of us would be next.

The CEO told us to sit down. We sat. He stood at the front of the room, arms folded. "If you disagree with my decision to fire him, I'm inviting you to hand in your resignation," he said, speaking slowly, as if he had rehearsed. He looked around the table, addressing each of us individually.

"Do you disagree with my decision?" he asked the account manager.

"No," the account manager said, raising his palms as if at gunpoint.

"Do you disagree with my decision?" the CEO asked the sales engineer.

"No," the sales engineer said. His eyelids fluttered. He looked ill.

"Do you disagree with my decision?" the CEO asked me. No, I said. But I did disagree; obviously, I disagreed. Whenever I wondered whether I had made the wrong decision, switching into the tech industry, Noah had served as my control. Discontent across the company was high, true—but I regularly looked around, saw him, and thought: It can't be that bad if *he's* still here.

After the meeting, we simmered in our unease. The job market was in our favor, we joked; better to get out while the company still looked good on our résumés. We brought a renewed commitment to our customer emails. We kept out of the way.

In the evening, some of us got ourselves out of the office and into a bar. We speculated about our job security, complaining about the bureaucratic double-downs, casting blame for roadblocks and poor product decisions. We talked about our IPO like it was the deus ex machina coming down from on high to save us—like it was an inevitability, like our stock options would lift us out of our existential dread. Realistically, we knew it could be years before an IPO, if we were bound for an IPO at all; we knew in our hearts that money was a salve, not a solution.

We were starting to realize that we had been swimming in the Kool-Aid; we were coming up for air. We were lucky and in thrall and then, unseen to us, we had become bureaucrats, punching at our computers, making other people—some kids—unfathomably rich. Maybe we never were a family. We knew we had never been a family. But maybe the CEO *was* just in it for the money. No, my teammates said—power. Power seemed right; we could agree on power.

We focused on staying hopeful. We reassured ourselves that this was just a phase; every startup had its growing pains. The problem, we discussed between drags on cigarettes, was that we did care. We cared too much. We cared about one another. We even cared about the CEO, who made us feel like shit. We wanted a good life for him, just like we wanted good lives for ourselves: we hoped he would get the chance to experience his own messy, reckless, ambivalent twenties. We didn't acknowledge that he might not want that for himself—he wasn't like us, didn't envy us, didn't care.

Eventually we were drunk enough to change the subject, to remember our more private selves: the people we were on weekends, the people we had been for years. We talked about where we'd once imagined ourselves at this stage. More stable, less anxious. More in control. We wanted power, too.

We threw our dead cigarettes on the sidewalk and ground them out under our toes. Phones were opened and contract drivers summoned; we gulped the dregs of our beers as cartoon cars approached onscreen. We dispersed, off to terrorize sleeping roommates and lovers, to answer just one, two more emails before bed.

Eight hours later, we were back in the office, slurping down coffee, running out for congealed breakfast sandwiches. Tweaking mediocre scripts and writing halfhearted emails, throwing weary and knowing glances across the table.

B eing the only woman on a nontechnical team, providing customer support to software developers, was like immersion therapy for internalized misogyny. I liked men—I had a brother. I had a boyfriend. But men were everywhere: the customers, my teammates, my boss, his boss. I was always fixing things for them, tiptoeing around their vanities, cheering them up. Affirming, dodging, confiding, collaborating. Advocating for their career advancement; ordering them pizza. My job had placed me, a self-identified feminist, in a position of ceaseless, professionalized deference to the male ego.

From time to time, the women in the office would go out to a nearby wine bar with fake fireplaces and plates of sweating charcuterie, and try to drink it out. I enjoyed these outings, even if they bore the metallic taste of duty—less a support network than a mutual acknowledgment. The other women were smart, ambitious, and a little quirky. One, a new account manager, worked on a treadmill desk and led a daily series of midafternoon crunches and push-ups to combat enervation and get our endorphins flowing. She was also a poet, I learned, which excited me. We should have gotten along better than we did, but it seemed impossible to bring our outside interests into work: they felt out of place and a little sad, like an outfit that looks put-together and chic at the beginning of the day but preposterous and overreaching by dusk.

I often wondered what work was like for our communications director, who was in her mid-thirties and had come through the investors. She was vastly more experienced than anyone else at the company, and far too professional to gossip or complain. She left the office every day at 5:00 to pick up her kids, and I suspected she was penalized for this: marketing and communications did not grow with the rest of the startup. There was no one else on the team. The CEO kept a drawing of himself, made by one of her children, pinned to a corkboard next to his workstation.

Other women I knew who worked in male-dominated offices all had unique coping strategies. Some took it as an opportunity to educate and course-correct. Some liked to scare and shame their colleagues for unabashed sexism. Others enjoyed the power play of workplace flirtation. One friend told me she regularly made fun of her CEO for having a gigantic dick, which she had discovered after sleeping with him. "Just inhabit your sexual power," she advised. "And use it to fuck with them."

If I had any sexual power, I didn't want to inhabit it in the office. I just wanted to keep up. There was one small exception: whenever we went out drinking, the account manager would, without fail, turn to me at the end of the night and ask me to slap him across the face. I knew it probably carried some sexual gratification for him, but I didn't care—it was very cathartic. It wasn't like he was asking me to spit in his mouth.

I wanted the men on my team to think I was smart and in control, and to never imagine me naked. I wanted them to see me as an equal—I cared less about being accepted by men sexually than I did about being accepted, full stop. I wanted to avoid, at all costs, being the feminist killjoy.

The Engineering team recruited a back-end developer straight out of a top undergraduate program: our first female engineer. She walked confidently into the office on her first day, springy and enthusiastic, carrying a leather purse that was not large enough to hold a laptop. I admired this: setting expectations by accessory.

The engineer's onboarding buddy brought her around to make introductions. As they approached our corner, the account manager leaned over and cupped his hand around my ear: as though we were colluding, as though we were five years old. "I feel sorry," he said, his breath moist against my neck. "Everyone's going to hit on her."

I was the feminist killjoy. I did not pick my battles. I died on every available hill. I asked my coworkers to stop using words like "bitch" in the company chat room. I bitched about being one of six women at a company of fifty. I wondered aloud if perhaps it was inappropriate to converse in graphic detail about app-enabled threesomes in the open-plan office. I stopped wearing dresses, to stanch a recruiter's stream of strange and unsettling compliments about my legs, which he spoke about as if I were a piece of furniture. A chair without a brain. A table with shapely legs.

Sexism, misogyny, and objectification did not define the workplace—but they were everywhere. Like wallpaper, like air.

The Account Management team brought on a man who spoke in inscrutable jargon and maintained a robust fleet of social media accounts; he had thousands of followers, and behaved as if he were an influencer. He was constantly changing his job title on a website where people voluntarily posted their own résumés, giving himself promotions to positions that did not exist. He told us, with some reluctance, that he was in his early forties. Age discrimination was crazy in this industry, he said. Local cosmetic surgeons were making a mint.

The influencer brought a scooter into the office and rolled around barking into a wireless headset about growth hacking: *value prop, first-mover advantage, proactive technology, parallelization. Leading-edge solutions. Holy grail.* It was garbage language to my ears, but customers loved him. I couldn't believe that it worked.

One afternoon, he rolled up to my desk. "I love dating Jewish women," he said. "You're so sensual." How did he know I was Jewish, I wondered, but of course he knew I was Jewish: large aquiline nose, gigantic cartoon eyeballs, eyelashes long enough to smash against the lenses of my glasses. I had the zaftig figure and ample rack characteristic of my sensual Ashkenazi kin. What did he want me to say, I wondered—*thanks*? Jewish people really value education, I mumbled.

I brought the comment up to the solutions manager during one of our perambulating one-on-one check-ins. I wasn't trying to get anyone in trouble, I said, as we walked past a sandwich shop effusing artificial bread scent, and the comment was not in and of itself so offensive—but I had to think about the influencer's sexual proclivities in the middle of my workday, and I wanted not to do that.

I felt guilty even mentioning it: the solutions manager didn't want to think about his team members' sexual proclivities either.

We turned in to a corporate park with a brutalist fountain. I had a brief fantasy about lowering myself into the basin and floating away. I remembered the conversation we'd had in which he had told me the company wanted to keep me, and my horrifying response: *Thank you*, I'd said. *I'd like to be kept.* I remembered his criticism, that I was a pleaser. I wanted to be less of one. I did not know how.

The solutions manager seemed embarrassed. "I'm sorry that happened," he said, staring at the sidewalk. "But you know him. That's just who he is."

At Christmas, the analytics startup rented out the newspaper-themed bar around the corner. The party was called for 4:00 p.m.; we carried our dress clothes into work and cleaned up in the office bathroom, like middle-school students preparing for a dance in the gymnasium. We were excited and exhausted, ready to celebrate.

I had already discussed with some of the women just how inappropriate was appropriate, and while others had dressed normally, I went conservative. I wore a black collared dress, black tights, and black boots, feeling vaguely like I was in an offensive Halloween costume: sexy Mennonite; naughty Lubavitcher. One of the newer account managers, taking pity on me, shellacked my hair into ringlets. I watched in the mirror as she traced halos of hair spray around my head.

It was disorienting to see my colleagues in formal wear. I had met most of my coworkers' significant others, but some were a mystery. I was delighted to see the exercise-fanatic account manager curled into the arm of a man wearing barefoot sneakers with articulated toes.

Cocktails in hand, the CEO and technical cofounder stood onstage, between parted velvet curtains, and gave a speech about how far we'd come. "A special thank-you," they said, extending their glasses, "to the partners and spouses." The partners and spouses, who had left their own jobs early to attend, clapped politely and chastely kissed the cheeks of their counterparts. I was glad that Ian was running late.

We traveled to a Michelin-starred restaurant, which the startup had also bought out for the night. Silent and dark-suited waiters served us Dungeness crab and seared black sea bass, Wagyu beef and lobster potpie, bottles of wine. The bar was open. People made out with their dates in a photo booth, unaware that it was digital—the photos would all be sent to the operations manager the next morning. Energy shots and lines of cocaine materialized in the bathroom. We danced against the glass windows of the restaurant—napkins strewn on the tables, shoes torn off—avoiding eye contact with the waitstaff.

People spilled out onto the sidewalk to smoke. I took a break from dancing and found Ian sitting alone, savoring his dessert. "This is one of the most memorable meals I've ever had in my life," he said, scraping his spoon along the edge of the plate. Desserts had been placed carefully in front of every setting, and they sat uneaten, discarded. I felt grateful for Ian, and ashamed. I had slipped so easily into a smug sense of belonging. I'd been so busy eating, drinking, performing my entitlement, that I hadn't even tasted the food.

As winter rolled on, it should have rained. Eventually, it did, if just barely. At the analytics startup, people had been hoping for a downpour, even though the city fell apart in the face of inclement weather: public transportation slowed or stopped altogether, and people behaved as if it were a holiday, sleeping in and arriving late, signing in to work from their apartments. Standing around in the kitchen, waiting for our sneakers to dry, someone would remark upon the bad traffic, or how long the bus had taken. "But," someone else would inevitably, dutifully counter, in acknowledgment of global warming and statewide drought, "we need it. We need it."

I had silently hoped the drought would keep up. Rain in San Francisco meant snow in Tahoe, which meant the annual ski trip was a go. Much as I liked most of my coworkers, I was wary about weekending with them—not to mention the higher-ups. It seemed like more of a liability than a perk: there was so much potential to introduce new and uncomfortable dynamics into workplace relationships. I didn't really want to know what everyone looked like when they first woke up, or hear an engineering manager grunting in the bathroom. I didn't want to listen to chipper colleagues make the same joke about not being a morning person; I was not a morning person. I pictured myself falling on the slopes and needing help, or getting stuck on a chairlift and being forced to make small talk as our noses ran. There was too much space to demonstrate vulnerability, personhood.

I also resented that it seemed as if we had no choice: it was not DFTC to skip out on the off-site. This made it feel like mandatory vacation, mandatory fun. Though it was a reward, a treat, the company trip was scheduled for a three-day holiday weekend, what others in the workforce might have considered personal time.

We gathered in the office at seven in the morning, carrying paper cups of coffee and winter coats. The operations manager distributed lift tickets and ski-rental vouchers, and read out the car assignments. The cars belonged to employees who had volunteered to drive, but the management team wanted to encourage back-seat cross-pollination. We stuck to our seating assignments. We were meant to bond, so we would bond. The trip was free.

The caravan quickly split up. Our group stopped at a strip mall for bacon, eggs, and bread, sacks of crinkle-cut chips, thirty-racks of light beer and handles of dark liquor. We were on our own for most meals, except for a symbolic dinner on the final night that was intended to pay tribute to the startup's humble roots: the CEO and the technical cofounder would personally cook the entire company spaghetti and garlic bread, just like the lean times. Rolling a cart through the aisles, tossing in sugary cereal and protein bars, I had the distinct feeling of being on vacation with someone else's family.

The startup had booked a row of condominiums at a resort in South Tahoe, up against the lake. The rustic apartments were comfortably generic, with wood-paneled walls, permanently damp carpets, mismatched silverware, and assorted, cheery Americana. Despite the family-friendliness, however, we lacked the natural ease of blood relatives choosing to vacation together. The housing groups had been preassigned, without employee consultation. I liked some of my coworkers better than others, but was largely indifferent to the sleeping arrangements. There was one person I hoped not to bunk with: several weeks prior, I had split a cab with one of the men from the Solutions team, en route to our mutual neighborhood after a late night spent drinking at work. During the ride, his hand had slipped up the back of my shirt, and, when I shoved it away, down the waistband of my pants. I kept the conversation going, pushing his hands away, sliding toward the window. We hadn't talked about it since, and I hadn't mentioned it—there wasn't anything, or anyone, to tell. I considered him a friend. Still, I was glad to find that the bedroom door locked.

The first evening, I wandered the grounds with Kyle, a willowy front-end developer who had been Noah's referral. He was modest and wildly talented, and rumored to have had a windfall after being an early employee at a gaming company that made a viral farming simulator. Kyle was one of the most serene people I had ever met—I felt I was extending my life expectancy just by being around him—and in his spare time, he made spacey, beautiful video games that weren't designed for virality. In the office, we played pranks on each other, exchanged cryptic cartoons on sticky notes, built word ladders in the company chat room. We biked to and from work in tandem. I was sure that we were annoying to our coworkers, but I didn't care; it felt good to have a buddy, a source of comfort and delight.

We smoked a tiny joint, skipped stones, and walked down the beach, peering into the windows of an adjacent resort. We passed the hot tub, where the salespeople were drinking from plastic cups. I could hear the solutions manager asking the doctor about his tattoos, which spread across his chest and arms. I knew, watching them bob in the jets, how badly the doctor wanted whatever marginal leadership role I held on Support. I knew that he would get it.

At happy hour, we all convened in one of the condos, where an assembly line of account managers was busy preparing pigs in blankets. EDM played over an elaborately rigged stereo; later, people would dance on the couches, throw themselves across the room, and pull down a quilted American flag that hung patriotically from the beams. I sat down at a long table with the solutions manager, who had brought up a bag of board games and was immersed in a heated round of Scrabble with the doctor.

The CEO came in and announced that he was flipping the script: to allow the support team some leisure time, the engineers were to do our job instead. We'd spent the morning on the road and the day on the mountain, and the queue of customer tickets stretched out for hours. Already, most of us were drinking. Some had been drinking all afternoon. Though it wasn't clear if we were working as we partied or partying as we worked, the scene in the condo was one of good-natured frustration as the engineers struggled to explain their own product to our users. The boys on my team mocked the engineers, rolling their eyes and leaning over their keyboards to correct them. At the time, this division of labor was a gleeful respite, a reversal of the power structure. Later, however, I realized the implication: our job was so easy, anyone could do it. They could even do it drunk.

Business was a way for men to talk about their feelings. The internet was choked with blindly ambitious and professionally inexperienced men giving each other anecdote-based instruction and bullet-point advice. *10 Essential Startup Lessons You Won't Learn in School. 10 Things Every Successful Entrepreneur Knows. 5 Ways to Stay Humble. Why the Market Always Wins. Why the Customer Is Never Right. How to Deal with Failure. How to Fail Better. How to Fail Up. How to Debug Your Anger. How to Build Workarounds for Your Emotions. How to A/B Test Your Kids. 18 Platitudes to Tape Above Your Computer. Raise Your Way to Emotional Acuity. How to Love Something That Doesn't Love You Back.*

One afternoon, I wandered into a fast-food restaurant during lunch and found the CEO sitting by himself, eating a veggie burger and looking at his phone. I sat down and he slid his fries across the table. He was reading a book by one of our investors, he said. I was familiar with it. The book offered guidance on how to navigate the choppy waters of entrepreneurship and conquer the twin demons of self-doubt and external pressure. It spoke of learnings, battles, journeys. Every chapter opened with an epigraph from a rap song. The struggle was real.

The men whom the CEO seemed to admire were the same men whom all the other men in the ecosystem admired: entrepreneurs, investors, one another. Chief among them was a founder of the seed accelerator, an English computer scientist who was the startup ecosystem's closest thing to an intellectual. An aphorism generator who blogged prolifically, his rhetorical style was cool, rational, and unemotional. He pontificated, at length, on intellectual conformity. He was prone to making favorable comparisons between startup founders and great men of history: Milton, Picasso, Galileo. I didn't doubt his business insight, but I didn't know why he seemed to believe it qualified him as an expert on anything—everything—else.

I had compassion for anyone who was trying to figure it out, and there was a part of me that sympathized with the CEO: though he would never admit it, he must have been in over his head. Still, I couldn't imagine modeling my own life after that of a venture capitalist—couldn't imagine reading a book simply because a financial middleman I'd never met had recommended it. Of course, they weren't just figureheads to the CEO, who knew them personally.

The book was good, the CEO told me. If you like this, you'll love therapy, I did not say. I looked at his phone. He was on the first page of a chapter titled "Preparing to Fire an Executive."

"That's a coincidence," he said, meeting my eyes. "Don't take it too seriously, or seriously at all." Firing people was horrible, he told me. It was like going through a bad breakup, but worse—agonizing. I told him not to worry; it was just a book.

I couldn't have taken it seriously, anyway. As things were, the CEO was also the president and the chairman of the board. He oversaw Product, Engineering, Solutions, Marketing. He was the only true executive we had.

Noah and I met for drinks in SoMa, a few blocks from the office. The bar smelled like a deep fryer, and a fleet of motorcycles hung from the ceiling. I hadn't seen him since he had been fired, and I was nervous: What if he blamed me? We embraced like long-separated family members.

Noah looked happier—relieved. His Australian work boots had dirt on them. He was sleeping better, he said. He was thinking about opening a worker-owned bagel shop—cooperatives were the only ethical business model—and trying to remove the word "app" from his vocabulary. "Ap-pli-ca-tion," Noah said, correcting himself. "The abbreviation obscures that it's software." This was deliberate and nefarious, reflected in the colorful, cartoonish designs of even the most technically sophisticated programs. "We're not software!" he chirped. "We're your friends!"

I offered a debrief on the startup: growth was hard, revenue was flowing, Tahoe was weird, we missed him. We rehashed his firing in lurid detail. The office was starting to feel really claustrophobic and air-conditioned and sterile, he said. His job responsibilities hadn't changed. "I thought, If I'm going to do this job forever, I'd better be rich in five years," he said. "I wanted to get paid out. I was employee thirteen. I wanted to work there, I wanted to work hard, but I wanted to make sure at the end of it I had a significant percentage of the company."

I was reminded, not for the first or last time, that my stake in the company was minuscule. When I had signed the offer letter, the number of shares sounded high, but I hadn't known to ask the size of the option pool. In a decent acquisition, I might net ten thousand dollars. I pulled on my beer, hard.

Noah paused and looked up at the bikes, then back at me. "You could describe my position as totally unreasonable," he said. "Or you could say what I asked for was what I needed, which was just a shitload more than what they were willing to give."

In any case, he said, at least his conscience was clearer. I asked what he meant.

"Come on," he said. "We worked at a surveillance company." He brought up the NSA whistleblower, who was back in the media. More revelations were coming out—nearly two hundred thousand documents had been released. The surveillance apparatus was larger and more complex than originally reported, and Silicon Valley was deeply implicated. "I didn't think about it while I was working there, because the product is so business oriented," Noah said. "I didn't necessarily see it as a problem for society. Plus, I don't think I had the information that all the money from the internet comes from surveillance."

By surveillance, I clarified, was he just talking about ad tech? I found digital advertising annoying, but I had never thought of it as particularly malicious—though it was clear from our customer companies that free services usually meant users were being exploited in one way or another. The most straightforward way to exploit them, naturally, was through rapacious data collection.

"I don't see a difference between the two, functionally," Noah said. "We facilitated the collection of the information, and we have no idea how it will be used and by whom. For all we know, we could have been one subpoena away from collaborating with intelligence agencies. If the reports are accurate, the veil between ad tech and state surveillance is very thin."

I didn't know how to respond. I didn't want to correct him. It was perhaps a symptom of my myopia, my sense of security, that I was not thinking about data collection as one of the moral quandaries of our time. For all the industry's talk about scale, and changing the world, I was not thinking about the broader implications. I was hardly thinking about the world at all.

I went to the symphony with my friend Parker, a digital-rights activist I knew from New York. Parker worked for a nonprofit focused on digital civil liberties—privacy, free expression, fair use—that had been founded in the nineties by utopian technologists with a cyberlibertarian bent. It was, in a sense, the ecosystem's anchor to history. The office was cluttered with dusty servers and outdated computers running creaky open-source software. People who really cared about technology, he had once explained to me, never used anything new. The default attitude was distrust.

Years prior, we had conducted an off-again, on-again, casual noncommitment, which had mostly consisted of him explaining things and then apologizing. "Email is about as secure as a postcard," he'd remind me, as we wandered between families at the farmers market in Fort Greene Park. "You don't expect your mailman to read it, but he could." I had listened patiently as he tried to teach me about cryptocurrencies and the promise of the blockchain, the shortcomings of two-factor authentication, the necessity of end-to-end encryption, the inevitability of data breaches.

The romance didn't last, but in its wake we had fallen into a rhythm of exchanging insecure emails on niche topics, like 1980s interface design, binary code, and public-domain art, and occasionally meeting for chaste, geriatric cultural activities.

The concert hall was a quarter full. As the lights dimmed, I made a silent promise that I would spend more time and money at San Francisco's older cultural institutions. I would participate in the civic life of the city where I lived. I would surrender my New York State driver's license. I would look up who the mayor was.

During intermission, we drank plastic cups of white wine and split a bag of candy. Parker was stressed about the erosion of net neutrality. He was working on a campaign to galvanize tech workers, but it wasn't gaining traction the way he had thought it would. I knew something about net neutrality already, but I let him explain it to me anyway. Nostalgia; old times' sake.

The problem, he said, was that the most important issues facing the tech industry were also the most tedious. It was in their interest to fight, but founders and tech workers didn't know how to organize. They didn't have the patience to lobby. They didn't consider their work political. "They all assume this will just last forever," he said.

We watched an elegant older couple drift by, properly dressed for a night out. I felt a little guilty for ruining their scenery. "The worst part," Parker said, "is that the technology is getting worse every day. It's getting less secure, less autonomous, more centralized, more surveilled. Every single tech company is pushing on one of those axes, in the wrong direction."

My throat felt like acid. Hey, I said, and paused. Parker looked over at me. Sugar dotted his lower lip. Do you think I work at a surveillance company? I asked.

"What a great question," he said. "I thought you'd never ask."

The startup was moving into the enterprise. We were selling to major corporations in and outside of the tech sector. We were selling to the United States government. We were becoming accountable.

The company was growing. There was never any coffee. We stood by the machine territorially, watching it brew. The operations manager installed a surveillance camera in the kitchen, posting screenshots to the company chat room of trespasses against the commons: dirty hands stuffed into the buckets of pretzels and chips, chocolate plucked out of the trail mix, bowls of milk and cereal poured into a backed-up sink. When I slipped and projectile-spilled a bucket of granola, the footage immediately entered the company record as an animated GIF.

The office was teeming with salespeople: well-groomed social animals with good posture and dress shoes, men who chuckled and smoothed their hair back when they couldn't connect to our VPN. They booked up the conference rooms, annexed the server closet, took calls in the stairwell. Their desks were scattered with freebies from our customers, stickers and beer sleeves and flash drives. Their base salaries were rumored to be more than twice what the support engineers were paid. They'd chosen cash over equity and, as such, were not to be trusted.

As early employees, we were dangerous. We had experienced an early, more autonomous, unsustainable iteration of the company. We had known it before there were rules. We knew too much about how things worked, and harbored nostalgia and affection for the way things were. We didn't want to outgrow the company, but the company was outgrowing us. None of us had anticipated that success would be to the detriment of what made the place feel special—what made it feel like ours. The new employees treated it like any other job. The new employees had no idea.

"Our culture is dying," we said to one another gravely, apocalyptic prophets toasting bagels in the company kitchen. "What should we do about the culture?"

It wasn't just the salespeople, of course. The salespeople were both consequence and harbinger. Our culture had been splintering for months. The CEO wouldn't stop using the word "paranoid." Our primary investor had funded a direct competitor. This was what investors did, but it still felt personal: Daddy loved us, he just loved us less. We feared it was slash-and-burn season. We feared we'd been hiring our own replacements all along. There was the sense of something looming.

Still, the weeks ticked past without incident. Every Tuesday afternoon, the emergency-warning siren heralded good news: for our revenue, our investors, our valuation, and, ostensibly, for us.

•

My meeting had no calendar invite, no warning. On a Friday afternoon, as I was packing up to leave, the CEO summoned me into a conference room.

"I thought you were an amazing worker at first," he said, palms on the table, voice slow. "Working late every night, last out of the office. But now I wonder if the work was just too hard for you to begin with."

He wanted to know: Was I Down for the Cause? Because if I wasn't Down for the Cause, then it was time. We could do this amicably. I stared at the four sculptural metal letters perched on a ledge at the end of the conference room: *D, F, T, C.*

I told him I was down—of course I was down. I tried not to swivel in my ergonomic chair. I cared deeply about the company, I said. I meant it. It did not occur to me to defend myself, to point out that the quality of my work had not changed. I was good at my job. The meeting was a hit—something to scare me. It worked.

If I didn't want to stay at the company, the CEO said, he would personally help me find a new job. Either way, I would not be leading the Support Engineering team. "I've decided you aren't analytical," he said. "I don't think we have the same values. I don't even know what your values are."

Of course I'm analytical, I thought. I might not have been a systems thinker, but I could deconstruct to death. I had thought we shared some of the same values, at least on their face: we were similarly disenchanted by corporate hierarchies, we liked underdogs, we both called ourselves feminists. We liked winning.

Despite my best efforts, I cried twice in the meeting, leaving in the middle to grab tissues from the bathroom, dodging looks of concern from the Engineering cluster. I leaned against the sink and wiped my face with a paper towel, as I had seen every other woman at the company do at one point or another. I thought about my friends back in New York. I thought about how hard I'd worked and how demoralizing it was to be told I had failed. I thought about my values, and I cried even more.

Back in the conference room, the CEO waited patiently. His face was unchanged when I returned.

In pursuit of higher truths, Ian and I drove up to Mendocino to do ecstasy. Using the home-sharing platform, we booked a guest suite in the home of an older couple who seemed to spend their days shouting at each other across the gulf of their gigantic sunken living room. The suite looked out across a valley: a bowl of fog. The landscape dripped.

While neither of us had much experience with controlled substances, Ian at least trusted the process. I trusted nothing. I sat on the bathroom sink and read pages of user-generated comments on a web forum dedicated to trip documentation. I looked up the location of the nearest hospital. Then I removed work email from my phone, making it impossible to reach the CEO or anyone else I might regret contacting while artificially flooded with serotonin.

We took the drugs and drank orange juice. We lay on a couch and listened to the cottony echoes of the older couple in the main house. We put on a Karen Dalton album and rubbed each other's backs and shared revelations about our families. I told Ian my worst secrets and felt content. I didn't feel high, or ecstatic— just like myself, but the good parts. Myself, but less anxious, less afraid. I wanted to replicate the experience with everyone I loved. This was my higher calling, I thought: sitting in a beautiful place, talking. I wanted to video-chat all my friends at once.

Life shone in its simplicity. I thought about the sweep of history, the improbability of convergence. Nothing seemed impossible. I had moved to California to accelerate my career, and now I was living through a historical inflection point, I effused—*we* were living through a historical inflection point. Ian had put on sweatpants and was stretching, happily, in front of a mirror. This was the new economy, the new way to live, I said—we were on the glimmering edge of a brand-new world, and we were among the people building it. Well, he was among the people building it. But I was *helping*.

I didn't know if I believed everything I was saying, but it felt so good to say it. "Very inspiring," Ian said, beaming. "You should give a keynote. New career: futurist."

The next morning, we drove to a hot spring and floated naked in a sulfuric pool with people whose bodies had begun to betray them. A wooden sauna vibrated with white-haired white people singing Native American folk songs. I wanted to live forever. I wanted to see what happened.

As we slid back into the city, the afterglow fading into a comedown, we talked about what came next. Ian encouraged me to quit my job. I gave the analytics startup as much space in my life as it asked for, and then some, he said. Work was making me miserable. He reminded me that it wasn't normal to cry in the office bathroom.

I explained that I felt a sense of loyalty. I wanted to prove myself to the CEO. I wanted to prove him wrong.

"He doesn't care about you," Ian said. "You're the smallest problem in his life. You're allowed to quit. He'll be fine."

It wasn't the first time Ian had initiated this conversation. It was always well-intentioned, but the unsolicited advice made me bristle, and not only because I refused to admit that he might be right.

As a software engineer, Ian had never encountered a job market with no space for him; he didn't know what it felt like not to have mobility, options, not to be desired. He loved what he did and could easily command three times my salary. No company would ever neglect to offer him equity. He was his own safety net.

I was perhaps still afflicted by the shortsightedness of someone whose skill set was neither unique nor in high demand. A sense of my own disposability had been ingrained since working in the publishing industry, and quitting without a plan was unfathomable. Every month since graduation was accounted for on my résumé. Sabbaticals, for anyone other than a college professor, were a novel concept, and one I could not trust.

Ian loved me in the way you love someone at the very beginning: he still believed I was the sort of person who wouldn't allow herself to be treated badly, to be made to feel like shit. Someone righteous, moral. Someone who valued herself. I empathized with his disappointment. I wanted to be that person, too.

Down for the Cause—what was the cause? Our cause was the company, but the company had causes, too. Driving engagement; improving the user experience; reducing friction; enabling digital dependency. We were helping marketing managers A/B test subject-line copy to increase click-throughs from mass emails; helping developers at e-commerce platforms make it harder for users to abandon shopping carts; helping designers tighten the endorphin feedback loop.

Helping people make better decisions, we had always said. Helping people test their assumptions. Answer tough questions.

Eliminate bias. Develop best-of-breed message targeting. Increase conversions. Improve key business metrics. Measure user-adoption strategy. Prioritize impact. Drive ROI. Growth-hack. What gets measured gets managed, I sometimes told customers, quoting a management guru whose writing I had never read.

The endgame was the same for everyone: Growth at any cost. Scale above all. Disrupt, then dominate.

At the end of the idea: A world improved by companies improved by data. A world of actionable metrics, in which developers would never stop optimizing and users would never stop looking at their screens. A world freed of decision-making, the unnecessary friction of human behavior, where everything—whittled down to the fastest, simplest, sleekest version of itself—could be optimized, prioritized, monetized, and controlled.

Unfortunately for me, I liked my inefficient life. I liked listening to the radio and cooking with excessive utensils; slivering onions, detangling wet herbs. Long showers and stoned museum-wandering. I liked riding public transportation: watching strangers talk to their children; watching strangers stare out the window at the sunset, and at photos of the sunset on their phones. I liked taking long walks to purchase onigiri in Japantown, or taking long walks with no destination at all. Folding the laundry. Copying keys. Filling out forms. Phone calls. I even liked the post office, the predictable discontent of bureaucracy. I liked full albums, flipping the record. Long novels with minimal plot; minimalist novels with minimal plot. Engaging with strangers. Getting into it. Closing down the restaurant, having one last drink. I liked grocery shopping: perusing the produce; watching everyone chew in the bulk aisle.

Warm laundry, radio, waiting for the bus. I could get frustrated, overextended, overwhelmed, uncomfortable. Sometimes I ran late. But these banal inefficiencies—I thought they were luxuries, the mark of the unencumbered. Time to do nothing, to let my mind run anywhere, to be in the world. At the very least, they made me feel human.

The fetishized life without friction: What was it like? An unending shuttle between meetings and bodily needs? A continuous, productive loop? Charts and data sets. It wasn't, to me, an aspiration. It was not a prize.

Unwinding over wine and potato chips one evening, the CEO sat beside me at one of the office kitchen tables. "You've been with us for a year," he said. "I ask everyone the same thing. Has this been the longest or the shortest year of your life?"

Longest, I said. It was knee-jerk, sincere. His eyes narrowed, and he half laughed. At the end of the table, the solutions manager visibly eavesdropped.

"It's a trick question," the CEO said. "The right answer is both."

As my annual review rolled around, I found myself on the fence about whether or not to bring up the running list of casual hostilities toward women that added unsolicited texture to the workplace. The company had grown to sixty employees, eight of whom were women: a decent ratio for the industry. But I was idealistic. I thought we could do better.

Over email, I told my mother about the colleague with the smartwatch app that was just an animated GIF of a woman's breasts bouncing in perpetuity, and the comments I'd fielded about my weight, my lips, my clothing, my sex life. I told her about the list the influencer kept, ranking the most bangable women in the office.

It was tricky: I liked my coworkers, and I did my best to dish it back. I didn't have horror stories yet, and I preferred things stay this way. Compared to other women I'd met, I had it good. But the bar was so, so low.

My mother had worked for corporate banks when she was my age. I assumed she'd understand. I expected her to respond with words of support and encouragement. I expected her to say, "Yes! You are the change this industry needs."

She emailed me back almost immediately. *Don't put complaints about sexism in writing*, she wrote. *Unless, of course, you have a lawyer at the ready.*

I was promoted from Support Engineering into something the industry called Customer Success. I was a customer success manager, a CSM. All of a sudden, I had an acronym and enterprise accounts. I had business cards. The cards had my personal cell phone number on them, and the slogans ACTIONS SPEAK LOUDER THAN PAGE VIEWS and I AM DATA DRIVEN—the absence of a hyphen still drove me crazy—but I handed them out to anyone who would take one.

The Customer Success team was small: just me and a former account manager, a newly minted M.B.A. who dressed in button-down shirts and polished leather brogues. The solutions manager told me that he expected we would make a great team. I agreed—I liked the M.B.A. and his dry, cynical humor. "He's strategic," the solutions manager said, beaming. "And you love our customers."

Our customers. My inbox and personal voice mail were full of demands from entitled, stubborn unknown men. I thought about all the times over the past year that I had been underestimated, condescended to, dismissed. It was true that I enjoyed translating between the software and the customers. I liked breaking down information, demystifying technical processes, being one of few with this specific expertise. I liked being bossy. But the men—I did not love any of them.

With the promotion came a bump in equity. I still did not

know what the shares were worth, and I was afraid to ask the M.B.A. whether he had been offered more when we were promoted. It seemed safe to assume the answer was yes. After all, his work was seen as strategy, while my work was interpreted as love.

Still, even without the equity—speculative money, anyway, I reassured myself—I was twenty-six years old and making ninety thousand dollars a year. I went on the internet and purchased a pair of five-hundred-dollar boots that I knew were fashionable in New York but, it turned out, I was embarrassed to wear in San Francisco—they looked so professional. I donated a little to a reproductive-health-care nonprofit. I donated a little to a local organization that provided mobile toilets and showers to homeless people in my neighborhood. I bought a vibrator with a USB port, because it made me feel more technical. I enrolled in a gym with a saltwater pool that I knew I'd never have time to swim in, and booked an appointment with a hypnotherapist recommended by a crowdsourced reviewing platform. I spent two hundred dollars on a single session, hoping to stop biting my nails, during which I accidentally fell asleep and had an unerotic dream about the founder of the social network everyone hated.

The rest of my money went straight into a savings account. Okay okay okay, I reassured myself, hiding in the server room on bad days, reviewing my bank balance. Escape hatch.

In the spring, the startup released a new feature, a report called Addiction. Addiction graphs displayed the frequency with which individual users engaged, visualized on an hourly basis—like a retention report on steroids. It was an inspired product decision, executed brilliantly by the engineers. Every company wanted to build an app that users were looking at multiple times a day. They wanted to be sticky—stickiest. The Addiction charts quantified and reinforced this anxiety and obsession.

Our communications director had left for a larger tech company with well-established, family-friendly benefits and policies, and had not been replaced. With her departure, I became the de facto copywriter. When I asked for a raise to reflect the extra work, the request was flatly denied. "You're doing this because you care," the solutions manager said—and I must have cared, because I kept doing it.

To promote Addiction, I ghostwrote an opinion piece for the CEO that described, dryly, the desirability of having people constantly returning to the same apps, multiple times an hour. *Addiction allows companies to see how embedded they are into people's daily lives*, I wrote, like it was a good thing. The piece was published on a highly trafficked tech blog under the CEO's name, and on our company blog under mine.

The novelty of Addiction was exciting, but the premise made me uneasy. Most of the company was under the age of thirty, and we had been raised on the internet. We all treated technology like it was inevitable, but I was starting to think that there might be other approaches. I already tied myself in dopamine knots all too often: I would email myself a link or note, feel a jolt of excitement at the subsequent notification, then remember I had just triggered it. App addiction wasn't something I wanted to encourage.

The branding also vexed me. I knew multiple people who had decamped for pastoral settings to kick dependencies on heroin, cocaine, painkillers, alcohol—and they were the lucky ones. Addiction was a generational epidemic; it was devastating. The Tenderloin was five blocks away from our office. There had to be higher aspirations. At the very least, there were other words in the English language.

I brought up my qualms to Kyle. It was like nobody at the company had ever been around someone with even a casual drug habit, I said. It was like substance abuse was an abstract concept, something that they'd only read about in the papers, if any of them bothered to read the news in the first place. It wasn't just insensitive, but sheltered, embarrassing, offensive. We may as well call our funnel reports Anorexia, I said. Let's start calling churn rates Suicides.

Kyle listened patiently while I ranted. He took off his floral cycling cap and rubbed the back of his head. "I hear you," he said. "The question of addiction is a big thing in gaming. It's nothing new. But I don't see any incentive for it to change." He pushed the miniature skateboard under my desk back and forth with the tip of his sneaker. "We already call our customers 'users.'"

Being a customer success manager was more interesting than being a support engineer, but the title was so corny and oddly stilted in its pseudo-sincerity that I could not bring myself to say it out loud. This turned out to work to my advantage: when I changed my email signature to read "technical account manager" instead, it actually elicited a response from previously uncommunicative clients—always engineers, always founders, and, still, always men.

The work was similar to support, but less technical and oriented toward the enterprise: the big boys. We CSMs were custodians of mutually beneficial long-term relationships. I had a roster of accounts, high-paying tech companies and corporations looking to get a taste of the cutting edge. My job was to ensure that these accounts were getting the most from the tool. While this included helping new companies onboard—provided they were paying a certain amount—it was also the friendly way of saying I would be fired if I couldn't prevent churn.

Churn was customer drop-off: when a customer realized they didn't need a third-party product, or forgot to use the tool, or switched to a competitor. Getting bigger was both a blessing and a curse, in this respect. It meant that we were gaining, but it also meant that newer startups had us in their sights. Competitors were coming on the market—smaller, nimbler companies with fewer employees and fresher funding. They were able to offer pricing that we, as a slightly more bloated company, were reluctant to match. They had a higher tolerance for burn.

But churn wasn't just about pricing or shifting loyalties. As with any business-to-business product, it often arose from neglect, when companies were paying thousands of dollars every month for a tool they forgot could be helpful. This was always the most damning feedback, because it meant that we had been forgotten.

I would meet accounts at their offices—NDA at reception, snacks and flavored water in the conference room, views of the bay from the Engineering cluster—and they would explain, matter-of-factly, that they were paying too much for something their engineers could just build themselves. It wouldn't be as pretty, but they could roll their own—pull their own solution together. The online superstore had begun selling back-end infrastructure that made this especially easy. Ours was a great tool, our customers said, but they needed to get the cost down.

I had trouble arguing with people who needed to downsize, but I didn't mind going on-site to try. It always felt like a field trip. I went to well-established corporations and admired the casual, carefree air of people who only put in three hours of work a day. I went to startups and declined offers of iced tea and string cheese. I brought the linen blazer back out. I thought I had such authority.

I didn't know that customer success managers at other companies were usually young women who somehow didn't look dowdy in floral prints and never left the house with wet hair, whose socks always matched, who didn't make too many jokes, who always knew the answers. Women who were much better at the job than I was—far more persuasive. Women to whom saying no was impossible.

It was easy to say no to me. I was always picking lint off my own chest, trying to skate by on good humor. When I met with customers, I acted like I was cosplaying a 1980s business manager. I said things like, Tell me what you want from your data, and Let's define your North Star metric. The North Star metric was always the same: whatever brought in money—as much of that as possible. I sat in conference rooms and reclined in comfortable chairs and tried to cultivate an aura of expertise. It was unclear whose mannerisms I had assumed, what fantasy I was channeling.

Though I knew I was unconvincing, the performance still seemed to work. It was reassuring to remember that the jobs we all had were fabrications of the twenty-first century. The functions might have been generic—client management, sales, programming—but the context was new. I sat across from engineers and product managers and CTOs, and thought: We're all just reading from someone else's script.

I skimmed recruiter emails and job listings like horoscopes, skidding down to the perks: competitive salary, dental and vision, 401(k), free gym membership, catered lunch, bike storage, ski trips to Tahoe, off-sites to Napa, summits in Vegas, beer on tap, craft beer on tap, kombucha on tap, wine tastings, Whiskey Wednesdays, Open Bar Fridays, massage on-site, yoga on-site, pool table, Ping-Pong table, Ping-Pong robot, ball pit, game night, movie night, go-karts, zip line. Job listings were an excellent place to get sprayed with HR's idea of fun and a twenty-three-year-old's idea of work-life balance. Sometimes I forgot I wasn't applying to summer camp. *Customized setup: design your ultimate workstation with the latest hardware. Change the world around you. We work hard, we laugh hard, we give great high fives. We're not just another social web app. We're not just another project-management tool. We're not just another delivery service.*

I got a haircut. I took personal time. I shrugged off the salespeople's knowing looks whenever I came into the office wearing anything dressier than a T-shirt and jeans.

I knew, from visiting my accounts, that startup offices tended to look the same—faux-midcentury-modern furniture, brick walls, snack bar, bar cart. When tech products were projected into the physical world they became aesthetics unto themselves, as if to insist on their own reality: the office belonging to the home-sharing website was decorated like rooms in its customers' pool houses and pieds-à-terre; the foyer of a hotel-booking startup had a concierge desk replete with bell (but no concierge); the headquarters of a ride-sharing app gleamed in the same colors as the app itself, down to the sleek elevator bank. A book-related startup held a small, sad library, the shelves half-empty, paperbacks and programming manuals sloping against one another. It reminded me of the people who dressed like Michael Jackson to attend Michael Jackson's funeral.

But one office, of the blogging platform with no revenue model, was particularly sexy. This was something that an office shouldn't have been, and it jerked my heart rate way, way up. There were views of the city in every direction, fat leather love seats, electric guitars plugged in to amps, teak credenzas with white hardware. It looked like the loft apartment of the famous musician boyfriend I thought I'd have at twenty-two but somehow never met. Being in the space made me want to take off my dress and my shoes and lie on the voluminous sheepskin rug and eat fistfuls of MDMA, curl my naked body into the vintage ball chair, never leave.

It wasn't clear whether I was there for lunch or an interview, which was normal. I was prepared for both and dressed for neither. My guide led me through the communal kitchen, which had the trappings of every other startup pantry: plastic bins of trail mix and cheese crackers, bowls of chips and miniature candy bars. There was the requisite wholesale box of assorted energy bars, and in the fridge were bottles of flavored water, string cheese, and single-serving cartons of chocolate milk. It was hard to tell whether the company was training for a marathon or having an after-school snack. But it wasn't unfamiliar— just a few days prior, I had walked into the analytics startup's kitchen to find two account managers pounding chewy cubes of glucose marketed to endurance athletes.

Over catered Afghan food, I met the team, including a billionaire who had made his fortune from the microblogging platform. He asked where I worked, and I told him.

"I know that company," he said, tearing a piece of lavash in two. "I think I tried to buy you."

Courtside seats to other startups' volatile trajectories had made me jaded, picky. Not that picky—I just wanted to work for a company that was innovative, rather than opportunistic, with a stable revenue model and a mission I could get behind. Maybe another pickax, but a normal business would be fine. Something useful. Somewhere I could take a breath, take stock.

A friend worked for a startup that made tools for developers— software for software engineers, to help them build more software—and she spoke highly of the work-life balance. The company was famous: everyone, from Silicon Valley's office park incumbents to the United States government, used its products, which made it simple for programmers to store, track, and collaborate on source code. The company also operated a public platform with millions of open-source software projects, which anyone could contribute to or download for free. Excitable tech journalists sometimes referred to this platform as the Library of Alexandria, but for code.

"I'm not trying to poach you, but it seems obvious to me

you would be a great fit," my friend told me over lunch, while extolling the virtues of her employer: two hundred employees, no real competitors, a hundred million dollars in funding. She dipped a french fry into her milkshake. "If you wanted to run a team, that's something that could happen. You could try it on, see what works for you." It all sounded so relaxed.

Things had not ended well for the Library of Alexandria, but I was still intrigued. The company had a real business model—selling private and self-hosted versions of the platform to corporations that wanted to apply the collaborative, open-source approach to proprietary software—and the public, free website struck me as radical. It offered unfettered access to the tools, knowledge, and online communities of the elite: a defensible allocation of venture capital. The startup glittered with idealism and old-school techno-utopianism. It was a corner of the industry that I found optimistic, experimental, and, most important, redemptive of the whole enterprise. I could see how it might actually make the world a better place.

There was, of course, a red flag. That spring, the startup had been implicated in a highly publicized gender discrimination scandal. The first woman on the engineering team—a developer and designer, a woman of color, and an advocate for diversity in tech—had posted a series of grievances to the microblogging platform. The startup, she claimed, was a boys' club, a sexist institution, down to the core: colleagues condescended to her, reverted and erased her code, and created a hostile work environment. She described a company culture where women were disrespected and intimidated.

The developer's posts went viral. The story wound its way up into the national media. The startup conducted an investigation. An implicated founder stepped down, and another moved to France. The venture capitalist who claimed software was eating the world took to social media to pledge his allegiance to the company.

All of this made me leery, but I also wondered, privately, if there might be some benefit to joining an organization immediately after this sort of blowup. I did not anticipate a matriarchal feminist utopia—based on the company's team page, about 20 percent of the employees were women—but I pictured a standard-issue boys' club deteriorating under the corrosive effects of chatter and public scrutiny. At the very least, I figured, employees would be talking about sexism openly. Sexism had to be part of the internal conversation. I'd read Foucault, a million years ago: discourse was probably still power. Surely, in the fallout, women would have a place at the table.

Call it self-delusion or naïveté; I considered these calculations strategic.

I took a personal day without giving a reason, an act of defiance that I feared was transparent, and scheduled an afternoon of interviews at the open-source startup. The office was a three-story former dried-fruit factory by the ballpark. In the reception area was a collection of glass museum cases showcasing artifacts from the company's history. I peered at a dented laptop that had belonged to one of the company's first engineers, and tried to feel moved. A security guard wearing a shirt with the company logo and the words SECRET SERVICE showed me to the waiting room and gestured toward a yellow couch. I took a seat, smoothed my hands over my lap, looked around, and dissociated.

The waiting room was a meticulous replica of the Oval Office, down to the wallpaper. The rug, a deep presidential blue, was emblazoned with the startup's cartoon mascot, an imaginary animal—a tentacled, doe-eyed octopus-cat crossbreed—holding an olive branch above the words IN COLLABORATION WE TRUST. An American flag stood to the side of the *Resolute* desk, behind which played an animation of clouds passing over the National Mall. White doors with precise, triangular molding led, presumably, to the West Wing.

This was peak venture capital, the other side of the ecosystem. The company appeared to be spending its hundred million dollars in venture funding the way any reasonable person would expect founders in their twenties to spend someone else's money: lavishly.

I didn't need to compare the office to the austere, fluorescent-lit tundra of the analytics startup, or even to Ian's cool, industrial-chic robotics warehouse, to appreciate the novelty of the work space. It was a fever dream, a fantasy, a playground. It was embarrassing, too giddy; more than a little much. When I entered a glass-walled, intimidating simulacrum of the White House Situation Room for my first interview, and saw that the boardroom table was flanked by two flags printed with the words IN MERITOCRACY WE TRUST, I laughed out loud. At each seat was a leatherette table pad embossed with the octopus-cat. It was all so literal.

Most surprising was that I liked it. The decadence excited me. What else happened here, I wondered—what else might employees get away with?

After months of being DFTC without once hearing the word "overtime," I was also thrilled by how the company appeared to rank on the ass-in-chair metric. By six in the evening, in the middle of the workweek, the office was dead quiet. With the exception of a half dozen employees pulling themselves beers and shaking cocktails at the bar, it was almost entirely empty.

I had the premonition that I would never again work in a

startup office that looked like it could be disassembled over-night, or in a culture-industry suite with mismatched coffee cups and drafty windows. I would not wear stretch-rayon business casual. I would not see mice. I would become self-actualized by achieving a healthy work-life balance, and I would allow myself to be taken care of, as if I had done something to deserve it.

If this was the future of work, I thought, then I was all in. I wanted every workplace to be like this—I wanted it for everyone. I believed that it was sustainable. I believed that it would last.

"We're expecting big things from you, ourselves, and for the company," read the offer letter, with condescension I found only vaguely objectionable. "You should be justifiably proud." I was, and I wasn't. Mostly, I was burned out.

The job offered top-of-the-line, fully covered insurance, partial 401(k) matching, and unlimited vacation, but it would entail a ten-thousand-dollar pay cut and a title demotion. For the time being, I wouldn't even be moving laterally; taking a typical customer support role was climbing down the ladder. This was an ill-advised move in any professional context, and especially naïve in the tech world: as an early employee of a promising startup, I could be leaving potentially high-value stock options on the table. But I didn't have stock options worth worrying about, and I didn't care about a huge payout, or titular glory—which was good, because the job title listed in the offer letter was, in homage to the company mascot, Supportocat. I set that humiliation aside.

What I wanted in a workplace was simple. I wanted to trust my manager. To receive fair and equal compensation. To not feel weirdly bullied by a twenty-five-year-old. To put some faith in a system—any system would do—for accountability. To take it all much less personally, and not get too close.

•

I called Parker. "Well, it's not ad tech," he said, deliberating. "So, that's good. And it's beloved by a lot of nerds. And the deal for working there, for any tech company, is so good right now. They'll make all the decisions for you. It's like going to a monastery, but better paid. The trade-off for that is you're not really encouraged to think about what you're doing. But you know that. I'm sure you've thought about that."

I had not really thought about that. But I believed in the mission, I told him. I didn't see the harm. I confessed that I thought the open-source platform had radical potential. Parker was quiet for a moment.

"For me, it's a dark specter of centralization," he said. "In a world without it, we could still do the things the platform allows, and people would be freer." He sighed. "But I'd prefer not to shame you, no matter where you go. There almost isn't a company you can work for that's good. Maybe a few nonprofits that aren't actively making things worse, but that's it. It's a very short list. Nothing you do is going to be more pernicious than the background radiation of SoMa."

I'm just going to take it, I said.

"Yeah," he said. "I know."

I scheduled a meeting to give notice. The solutions manager and I sat down in the Pentagon, and I offered the lines I had been rehearsing in my head: I learned so much, enjoyed my time, was grateful they had taken a chance on me. None of this was a lie. They had taken a chance on me. I had enjoyed my tenure, to a point. It had been an invaluable education.

The solutions manager leaned back in his chair and nodded. Around and around went the wedding ring. I knew that he had cried when he fired Noah, and I felt a little disappointed that he wasn't crying about me. He asked, perfunctorily, if there was anything that the company could do to get me to stay. I told him no, and we both seemed relieved.

I thought it was most dignified to personally tell the CEO I was leaving, like a protocol he might have read about in our VC's business book, but the solutions manager beat me to the punch. Throughout the day, I eyed the CEO, and he studiously ignored me. When I approached him, he turned on his heel, walking away while staring into the middle distance.

That evening, from the blissful isolation of one of the conference rooms, I saw the CEO striding across the office in my direction. Still avoiding eye contact, he entered the conference room, sat down, and told me he had heard my news. News: like I was pregnant, or dying, or important. I nodded and tried not to apologize. Like a high school drama student running lines, he thanked me for my work. "I'm sorry I made you cry that one time," he said to the window behind me.

I had not gotten to know him, I thought. We were not friends. We were never family. I did not understand the sacrifices he had made for the company, or how far he would go to protect it. I did not know what made him tick. There was a coldness that frightened me.

I reassured him that it was fine. This was a lie, but not for his benefit. I needed to believe it much more than he did.

At the end of August, I deleted personal files from my laptop and ate a final handful of trail mix. The operations manager was too overextended to conduct an exit interview, for which I was grateful. I had nothing left to contribute. I said a few overly sentimental farewells and signed more paperwork, none of which I fully understood without a lawyer present. It did not occur to me that I could ask for more time, or even say no.

After surrendering my badge, I biked away from the office, wild with possibility. My backpack, light without a work laptop, flapped against my spine as I cruised up Market Street. I felt liberated, discharged. In the Panhandle, I passed a group of runners in matching startup T-shirts, trotting through the eucalyptus like a string of well-broke ponies, and I pitied them.

That evening, Ian picked me up from home in a rental car, and we drove into Berkeley, snaking through the hills. We pulled over at a lookout and sat on a boulder, eating curried couscous and drinking cheap champagne. Across the bay, San Francisco flickered. Fog settled over the city, draping itself around the parks, the hills, the piers.

All this time, and I could just leave. I could have left months ago. For nearly two years, I had been seduced by the confidence of young men. They made it look so simple, knowing what you wanted and getting it. I had been ready to believe in them, eager to organize my life around their principles. I had trusted them to tell me who I was, what mattered, how to live. I had trusted them to have a plan, and trusted that it was the best plan for me. I thought they knew something I did not know.

I swam in relief. Watching the city, wrapped in Ian's jacket, I did not see that I was in good company: an entire culture had been seduced. I understood my blind faith in ambitious, aggressive, arrogant young men from America's soft suburbs as a personal pathology, but it wasn't personal at all. It had become a global affliction.

SCALE

The open-source startup was an institution. People had been collaborating on free software for decades, long before the founders, four fresh-faced programmers in their twenties, revolutionized—and monetized—the scene. The startup, however, made the process faster, more reliable, social. The platform genuinely improved the lives of developers, who were predisposed to simple, elegant solutions designed by people who thought just like they did. The company had been profitable practically from the get-go, and was a paragon of product-market fit: catnip for venture capitalists. The founders decided to do things differently. There was no one to tell them no.

The company was modeled on the free software community, with its subversive, countercultural, and deeply techno-utopian ethos. For years, in emulation of the tenets of open-source—transparency, collaboration, decentralization—the startup was flat. There was no hierarchy. There was no org chart. Employees had named their own compensation, determined their own priorities, and come to decisions by consensus. The founders did not believe in management, but in meritocracy: the best would naturally rise to the top.

Everyone was encouraged to work how, where, and when they worked best—whether that meant three in the morning in the San Francisco office, referred to as HQ, or from inside a hammock on Oahu. They were invited to bring their whole selves into work, and reminded to take their whole selves on vacation. Vacation, which was unlimited, was not tracked. Business hours did not exist. Half the workforce was remote, and digital nomadism was considered banal.

The company was obsessed with developers, and the feeling was mutual. Users displayed a level of brand loyalty that bordered on fanaticism. They tattooed the mascot onto their bodies and sent photos to Support, the skin raw and red, the ink still fresh. The web shop sold enough swag—branded clothing, stickers, barware, toys, infant onesies—that it could have been an independent business. Tour groups from around the world cruised through the office, taking selfies behind the *Resolute* desk and at the base of a six-foot statue in the lobby of the octopus-cat, cast in bronze and styled as *The Thinker*.

Some employees were well-known in the open-source community, as high-profile maintainers of popular repositories or authors of programming languages. Others leveraged the startup for personal acclaim, blogging and branding their way to minor celebrity. They traveled the world as self-appointed corporate evangelists, hopping continents on the infinite conference circuit. They talked programming frameworks in Tokyo, design thinking in London, the future of work in Berlin. They spoke with the authority of tenured professors to audiences of eager developers, designers, and entrepreneurs, seas of men yoked with laminated day passes. They gave inspirational talks about the toxicity of meetings and waxed poetic about the transcendence of collaboration. They parlayed their personal experiences into universal truths. When they dropped by San Francisco, they walked around SoMa wearing the employee hoodie, acting like people were going to recognize them. Sometimes, people did.

I spent my first week on the job lurking, reading internal message boards and paging through chat room back-scroll. Despite the opulence of HQ, the buildout of which was rumored to have cost ten million dollars, the true headquarters of a remote-first company was the cloud. To ensure that all employees were on equal footing regardless of geography, the majority of business was conducted in text. This was primarily done using a private version of the open-source platform, as if the company itself were a codebase. People obsessively documented their work, meetings, and decision-making processes. All internal communications and projects were visible across the organization. Due to the nature of the product, every version of every file was preserved. The entire company could practically be reverse engineered.

There were only two hundred employees, but the startup had, in a sense, built a private internet community. People referred to each other by their platform handles, both online and in person. Even the CEO signed off on emails and internal posts with his username. The corporate chat software lit up every few seconds with data, information, digital ephemera; it contained multitudes. There were channels for science fiction readers, comic book lovers, night owls, politics junkies. There was a channel for people to post photographs of dogs in the office, and a channel for people to post photographs of dogs they followed on social media. There were channels for barefoot-shoe enthusiasts, martial arts practitioners, recovering music majors. For people who loved karaoke, or basketball, or theme parks, or bland food, or sous vide machines. For people to talk about tiny homes. For knitters. Forty people belonged to a channel dedicated solely to the discussion of ergonomic computer keyboards.

My coworkers were fanatics for emojis and deployed them liberally, as a substitute for language and a lever for passive aggression. A tiny whale, a tiny ice-cream cone, a tiny, steaming pile of shit. A tiny custom octopus-cat; a tiny photo of the CEO's face. I was embarrassed by the thought of using my laptop in public spaces—my work looked like a video game for children.

The archive of institutional knowledge, however, was fascinating. Absent any formal onboarding program, I made up my own. I read chat history from the period when the gender discrimination accusations were first made public; transcripts from all-hands meetings addressing the scandal; discussion in the Human Resources repository. I saw how my coworkers had reacted in real time, and who had been quick to throw the first woman in Engineering under the bus. Reading back-scroll made me feel like a creep, but it was a useful research project, a means of discovering whom to avoid and whom to trust.

My second week, I flew to Chicago to participate in a hack house. Hack houses were a routine practice across the company: every few months, teammates would convene in a city of their choice—Austin, Athens, Toronto, Tokyo—and spend a few days catching up, planning, and drinking. My new coworkers, digital assimilationists if not digital natives, referred to this as getting together in meatspace.

The company had rented a mansion in the Gold Coast neighborhood, a sprawling Art Moderne villa that once belonged to a shoe heiress but had since been renovated and decorated with a garish minimalism that screamed porn set: geometric furniture, zebra rugs, white baby grand, and a full-sized stuffed steer. In my room, an en-suite bath was separated from the bed by half a wall of glass brick.

The first night, I pushed my duffel bag against the bedroom door, which did not lock. Sometime before dawn, I awoke to the sounds of a technical support engineer, a gentle aviophobe who had taken an eighteen-hour train from Colorado, shuffling into the building and crashing in the room across the hall. I emerged the next morning to find his door open; he lay facedown on the bed, limbs spread, snoring.

The Support team spent the daytime hours sprawled out on deep leather couches in the living room, talking about ordering takeout and making jokes in the chat channel while clearing the queue. In the evenings, the group monopolized top-rated New American restaurants for midwestern farm-to-table and traveled to black-box theaters for midwestern comedy. In the mornings, people woke up late and padded around the mansion in pajamas, frying bacon and responding to support tickets.

While a weeklong sleepover would not have been my first choice for meeting new coworkers, I felt fortunate. My teammates were good-natured, funny, laid-back. Almost all of them were older than I was, and about half were women. A good number had previously been employed as librarians or archivists, and were drawn to the open-source startup for reasons similar to mine: the utopian promise of free, easily distributed, well-organized knowledge; a livable salary; really good benefits.

My onboarding buddy, an earnest and thorough southerner who had previously worked at an education nonprofit, walked me through the internal ticketing software. The company's engineers were picky, I noted: even the support queue integrated with the open-source platform.

The ticketing software had been built by the first Supportocat, my onboarding buddy explained, and could be buggy. "Just ping him if anything breaks," she said, and gave me the developer's platform handle, a cute nickname that invoked a bear cub. What's his name, I asked, and my onboarding buddy smiled. "That is his name," she said. She leaned in confidentially. "He identifies as a tanuki, a Japanese racoon dog. Only the founders know his legal name." Oh, I said, feeling very vanilla. "He's at HQ sometimes," she said. "You'll know him by the tail."

On the second night, as we expensed nightcaps at a dive bar near the mansion, the mood turned, and the Supportocats started to talk shit. The company was struggling, my coworkers said—culturally, at least. The startup had enjoyed a prolonged awkward adolescence, and now it had to grow up. The founder who had left postscandal had been the lifeblood of the organization, and the CEO was well-intentioned but conflict averse. For the first time in the company's history, people were threatening to quit.

The employees were haunted by what had happened with the first woman engineer, my coworkers explained. Many had taken it personally. They'd been let down by people they considered to be family. They were heartbroken. They had been complicit, and hadn't even known. They were terrified it would happen again.

But also—it was complicated. "On the one hand, if we have a problem with sexism or sexual harassment, then that problem needs to be addressed," a teammate told me. "On the other hand, this hurt everyone." I asked what she meant, and she pushed her hair to the side. "I don't know if the company will ever recover from this," she said. "And, to put things bluntly, she wasn't the only one with equity."

Back in the office, there was a lot of chatter about a group of internet trolls who had mounted a harassment campaign against women in gaming. The trolls had flooded social networks, spouting racist, misogynistic, and reactionary rhetoric. They railed against feminists, activists, and those whom they dubbed, pejoratively, social justice warriors. They had been banned from nearly every other platform, and responded by citing the First Amendment and crying censorship. This caught the attention of some right-wing commentators and white supremacists, who offered endorsement and solidarity.

On the open-source platform, the trolls maintained a repository of resources and information on women they were targeting—photos, addresses, personal information—and outlined strategies for stalking, harassment, and media pressure. The accounts contributing to the repository were mostly sock puppets, tied to burner emails and using an overlay network to obscure IP addresses. The people behind them were unidentifiable and impossible to trace.

My coworkers debated how seriously to take the campaign. They were used to seeing social media weaponized in this way, they told me: trolls and shitposters existed on every platform, and were best flagged as spammers or ignored.

"If you spend five minutes in gaming communities, you'll see this sort of thing," a teammate said. I hadn't played a video game since I was a kid; I didn't know there were communities. "They're just a bunch of dudes in their parents' basements," he said. "They'll move on." Still, he admitted, looking at the repository of email templates and phone call scripts, it was unusual to see them so organized.

The company did not have a formal team to handle these sorts of situations. An ad hoc collection of executives, support representatives, lawyers, and rubberneckers had formed a casual decision-making chat room called Hazmat, to deal with occasional controversies and platform flare-ups. After weeks of internal discussion, inaction, and complaints from the community, the Hazmat group disabled the repository. Immediately, employees were mobbed on social media. The Support inbox was flooded with death threats.

I showed one of the engineers a particularly hostile message that had come into the queue. We looked up the email address in our admin tool, and found the associated account. The user profile had an avatar of a man with a thin mustache and wild eyes. "This is who you're worried about?" the engineer asked. "Come on. You know who these people are. Dakimakura pillows, holes front and back. You'll be fine. His mom's not going to drive him to a murder."

The engineer rolled back to his desk, and I opened a new tab and searched *dakimakura pillows*. The world was vast and unknowable, I thought, flipping through product photographs. I felt very innocent and naïve.

The people behind the sock-puppet accounts were just assholes, my coworkers said, dropping animated GIFs of eye-rolling celebrities into the chat room. They were immature or bored, probably students: the company always saw an uptick in abuse reports during school vacations and over long weekends. Just a bunch of bad actors, they reassured me, atypical for the platform—not worth any more time, not worth our engagement.

As an onboarding gift, the open-source startup gave all employees a step-count wristband: fit workers were happy workers, and probably cheaper to insure. I wore the wristband for a week, tracking my steps and calibrating my caloric intake, until I realized I was on the brink of an eating disorder.

The ecosystem's fetish for optimization culture and productivity hacking—distraction blockers, task timers, hermit mode, batch emailing, timeboxing—had expanded into biohacking. On the internet and in San Francisco's finer coffee shops, systems thinkers swapped notes about their stacks and dosages. They optimized their sleep cycles with red light and binaural beats. They bought butter-laced cold brew, shot up their thighs with testosterone, and purchased haptic-feedback wristbands to self-administer 150-volt electric shocks.

The body was a platform, the biohackers argued: if an upgrade was available for their laptop's operating system, they would download it posthaste, without question. The same was true of their human organisms. New companies sold nootropics, unregulated cognitive-enhancement drugs claiming to unlock next-level thinking, to those striving for peak performance.

I wanted to be above it, but I wasn't above it. Too curious; too wistful for my college roommate's ADHD medication. I ordered capsules of nootropics from a startup claiming to be manufacturing Human 2.0. The capsules weren't approved by the FDA, but the startup was funded by the same investors who paid my salary. I took them in anticipation of high productivity, but my thinking remained locked, maxing out at the usual level.

"I don't like this new phase," Ian said, inspecting the nootropics package. The capsules rattled in their glass jar, branded with a lightning bolt. "L-theanine? This is like what you get from a homeopath, just with flat design." He declined my offer of a mocha-flavored caffeine gummy.

There was something a little bit sad about body optimization, I thought, after accidentally spending an afternoon on nootropics in the bathroom with my eyelids taped, watching makeup tutorials and attempting to perfect a dramatic cat-eye. The goal was productivity, not pleasure. And to what end—whom did it serve? Perhaps gunning for high output in one's twenties was a way to compress the peak-of-life productive years, tee up an early retirement with a still-youthful body, but it seemed brazen to play God with time.

It seemed more likely that biohacking was just another mode of self-help, like business blogging. Tech culture provided endless outlets for men to pursue activities coded as female—including, apparently, body manipulation. I could see how tracking personal metrics offered a sense of progress and momentum, measurable self-betterment. Leaderboards and fitness apps encouraged community through competition. Quantification was a vector of control.

Self-improvement appealed to me, too. I could stand to exercise more often, and be more mindful of salt. I wanted to be more open and thoughtful, more attentive and available to family, friends, Ian. I wanted to stop hiding discomfort, sadness, and anger behind humor. I wanted a therapist to laugh at my jokes and tell me I was well-adjusted. I wanted to better understand my own desires, what I wanted; to find a purpose. But nonmedical monitoring of heart rate variability, sleep latency, glucose levels, ketones—none of this was self-knowledge. It was just metadata.

Going into work wasn't mandatory, but for a while I did it anyway. It was a pleasure to spend time at HQ, in the same way it would be a pleasure to kill a few hours in the lobby of a boutique hotel. There were vending machines stocked with new keyboards, headphones, cables, and cords, all of which tumbled down, free, with the tap of an employee badge. The elevators were never broken. An engineer was rumored to have lived in the office for a while, sleeping in a lounge area atop an indoor shipping container—a visual pun on shipping code— until he was discovered, by the security team, bringing home a date.

My coworkers treated it as much like an office as a clubhouse. People roamed around barefoot, juggling and playing guitar. They came in wearing expressive and ironic clothing: spandex leggings printed with unicorn emojis, shirts printed with teammates' faces, bondage collars, Burning Man pelts. Some played video games while they half worked, or napped in the coder caves—dark, cushioned booths designed for those who worked best under conditions of sensory deprivation.

It seemed like half of the engineers were DJs—a group of

developers regularly performed at a club in the Mission, with a data scientist who projected angular and geometric visualizations on a screen behind them. Some of them practiced on a mixer across from the company bar, reminiscing proudly about dance parties they had hosted in the office, and the times neighbors had threatened to call the cops.

Despite the robust amenities and club culture, the office was rarely full. Meetings were held over videoconferencing software, and people dialed in from wherever they happened to be: public transportation, pool loungers, unmade beds, living rooms with partners napping in the background. An engineer attended his daily stand-up meeting from an indoor climbing wall, gripping a plastic rock and wearing a harness. A telepresence robot rolled around the first-floor event space, lanky and conspicuous, a bridge between worlds.

People came and went, operating on individualized schedules. I never knew whom I would run into at HQ, or whether I would be working alone. On every floor were mounted television screens displaying heat maps, and lists of employee avatars indicating who was in the building and where. The heat maps felt like a violation—I didn't know how to opt out. I side-eyed the television monitors whenever I walked to the bathroom, waiting for my data, a radiant orange blob, to catch up. The maps almost offered a feeling of company cohesion. It was surprisingly affecting to be the only node.

I still wanted to be part of something. I staked out an unclaimed standing desk in a cluster of engineers, and left my new business cards next to the monitor: a flag in the ground. I decorated my laptop with octopus-cat stickers from the company store. I patronized the in-house masseuse and received a cautious, fully clothed back massage, the decadence of which left my body tense with shame. I drank scotch with coworkers in a room hidden behind the library bookcases and designed to look like a nineteenth-century smoking parlor: coatrack of velvet jackets, a globe that served as a stash box, and, above the mantel, an oil painting of the octopus-cat as Napoleon Bonaparte. I tripped over my own ankles on the company soccer team, doing my part to help meet the two-woman quota. I used the office gym and showered anxiously in the office locker room, deciding to never again get naked at work. I walked around proudly in my employee hoodie: my platform handle lettered down the sleeve, the silhouette of the mascot plastered over my heart.

I was employee number two hundred and thirty-something. At that point, the number didn't matter. I had no trouble identifying the early employees, and not just because some listed their hire numbers in their social media bios. I saw my former self in their monopolization of the chat rooms, their disdain for the growing nontechnical teams, their wistfulness for the way things had been.

I did envy these early employees, their inside jokes and well-deserved pride. Sometimes, reading their banter or seeing photos of their children dressed as the octopus-cat for Halloween—or skimming engineers' personal blog posts extolling the virtues of asynchronous collaboration and the Zen of open source— I would think about my foregone institutional authority, or the stack of data-driven T-shirts I kept folded beneath my towels, and feel a jolt of nostalgia. Desire. Corporate loneliness. I would yearn for the sense of ownership and belonging, the easy identity, the all-consuming feeling of affiliation. And then I would remind myself: *There but for the grace of God go I.*

•

Support met once a week, for an hour, over videoconference. I prepared for these meetings by brushing my hair, closing the curtains to the street, then frantically tossing visible clutter on top of my bed and covering it with a quilt.

"Maybe we should split your job," Ian suggested one morning, watching me position my laptop so that the laundry rack, draped with underwear, was out of frame. "We can both work part-time, live off one salary, and travel around the world. Who would ever know?" No one, I said. While we were at it, I told Ian, he might as well get us promoted into Engineering. I could do the video chats, and he could write the code.

While my teammates did fly out to HQ from time to time, it was strange when we were embodied, disorienting to see everyone from the neck down. Our relationships, fostered through software, did not immediately map onto physical reality. We were all more awkward in person than in the company chat rooms and over video, where conversation flowed.

I liked the specific intimacy of video: everyone breathing, sniffling, chewing gum, forgetting to mute the microphone before clearing their congestion. I liked the banter, the frozen mid-sentence faces, the surprise of seeing an animal emerging from under a desk. I liked watching everyone watch themselves while we pretended to watch one another, an act of infinite surveillance. The first ten minutes were almost always spent correcting the videoconference software, during which I became acquainted with my teammates' home interiors, their color-coded bookcases and wedding photos, their earnest letterpress posters or obscure art. I learned about their hobbies and roommates. I grew fond of their children and pets.

At the start of these meetings, I would log in and lean into my laptop, enjoying the camaraderie and warmth of a team. For an hour, my studio would fill with laughter and chatter, conversation tripping when the software stalled or delayed. Then I would stand up, stretch, tape back over my laptop camera, and open the curtains—adjusting to the silence, alone in my room.

The engineers all read a heavily moderated message board, a news aggregator and discussion site run by the seed accelerator in Mountain View. The message board was frequented by entrepreneurs, tech workers, computer science majors, libertarians, and the people who loved to fight with them. People whose default conversational mode was debate. Mostly men. Men on both sides of the seawall; men all the way down.

It wasn't for me, but I read it anyway. It struck me as the raw male id of the industry, a Greek chorus of the perpetually online. The site's creator had specified that political debate destroyed intellectual curiosity, so political stories, and political conversation, were considered off topic and verboten. Instead, the guidelines asked that users focus on stories that were interesting to hackers. I had always considered hacking an inherently political activity, insofar as I thought about hacking at all, but it seemed the identity had been co-opted and neutralized by the industry. Hacking apparently no longer meant circumventing the state or speaking truth to power; it just meant writing code. Maybe would-be hackers just became engineers at top tech corporations instead, where they had easier access to any information they wanted. Whatever; I wasn't a hacker.

The posters experimented with new ideologies they seemed to have discovered on crowdsourced wikis. In conversations about industry stories, white papers, product announcements, and one another's personal blog posts, they swapped notes about ethics, philosophy, and economics. *What books make up the core of your operating system?* the men asked one another, with great sincerity. They discussed how to preserve mental cycles, how to achieve a state of Deep Work. They debated the merits of a Hippocratic oath for developers, the existence of natural monopolies, the value creation of personal compliments, the state of the Overton window. They talked about Stoicism as a life hack. They teetered on the brink of self-actualization.

When news about the open-source startup's gender discrimination case first came to light, the message-board commentariat had grappled with the company's fall from grace. They pounced on a detail that had surfaced in the reports, about male employees watching their female coworkers Hula-Hoop to music in the office. The first woman in Engineering had described the employees ogling their colleagues, as if at a strip club. It's not like watching Hula-Hoopers would make men rapists, one commenter argued—after all, not even strip clubs turned men into rapists.

Should CEOs be allowed to bring employees to a strip club? someone asked. What if the employees initiate, and they're women, and *they* invite the CEO? Another man chimed in to suggest that the Hula-Hoopers were putting on a show—perhaps they wanted to be ogled. Remember, chided an ambassador from the land of evolutionary psychology: desire was an evolutionary imperative.

Side arguments had broken out about the forensics of re-
verting someone else's code. Some debated the role played by
the open-source startup's choice of programming languages.
Perhaps, they posited, the company's choice of language mir-
rored the workplace conditions. Someone pointed out that people
tended to confuse tech's gender ratio—worse than average, he
acknowledged—with its harassment rate, which was difficult to
judge compared to other industries.

*Men built a wildly successful company where they loved
to work, and now they have to destroy it to make feminists feel
welcome*, fumed a prolific commenter.

A man whose handle paid homage to a cartoon cat stirred
up a debate about the qualities of a positive office environment.
Why, he asked, *would a workplace filled with happy young males
necessarily be a bad culture?*

I flew to Phoenix for an annual conference of women in computing. The conference had been established in honor of a female engineer who helped develop military technologies during
the Second World War, a nod, perhaps inadvertent, to the industry's underacknowledged government origins. On the plane,
I joked with my seatmate about whether the National Security
Agency would have a recruitment booth: a bad joke that only
got worse when I learned that the NSA was one of the conference's major patrons.

I was not really a woman in computing—more a woman
around computing; a woman, with a computer—but I was curious, and the open-source startup was a conference sponsor.
All interested employees, regardless of gender, were invited to
attend. While nobody was excited to explore Phoenix, a city
whose downtown appeared to be a series of interconnected park-

ing lots, the company put us up in a boutique hotel with a pool and a Mexican restaurant. The restaurant bar quickly became our new headquarters.

On the first night, my coworkers gathered over bowls of guacamole and sweaty margaritas. For many of them, the conference was just an excuse to get together in person, a reunion of sorts. Many hadn't seen one another since the startup's gender discrimination crisis. There was a lot to catch up on.

I hovered on the periphery, hoping the women engineers would adopt me. I found them intimidating: smart, passionate about their work, and unafraid to call bullshit, at least in the privacy of their own cohort. Some of them had unnaturally colored hair and punk-rock piercings, signaling industry seniority as much as subcultural affiliation. I had no conception of what it would be like as a woman in tech whose skill set was respected. I was disappointed to learn that it wasn't too dissimilar from being a woman whose skill set wasn't.

For the most part, the other women seemed glad that some of the company's problems had been exposed. Too many people puking in the elevator, metaphorically and not. Too many unexamined disparities. The obsession with meritocracy had always been suspect at a prominent international company that was overwhelmingly white, male, and American, and had fewer than fifteen women in Engineering. For years, my coworkers explained, the absence of an official org chart had given rise to a secondary, shadow org chart, determined by social relationships and proximity to the founders. Employees who were technically rank-and-file had executive-level power and leverage. Those with the ear of the CEO could influence hiring decisions, internal policies, and the reputational standing of their colleagues.

"Flat structure, except for pay and responsibilities," said an internal tools developer, rolling her eyes. "It's probably easier to be a furry at this company than a woman."

"It's like no one even read 'The Tyranny of Structurelessness,'" said an engineer who had recently read "The Tyranny of Structurelessness."

It was perhaps predictable that modeling a company after an internet community would have drawbacks, but modeling a company after the open-source software community turned out to have been uniquely fraught. On top of the problems with meritocracy and the no-managers workflow, open source was historically a boys' club. Fewer than 5 percent of contributors were women. Exclusionary rhetoric proliferated. Even in person, at technical meet-ups and conferences, men pontificated and strutted across stages with pop-star lighting while the women engineers were leered at, condescended to, groped. *Can't get sexually harassed when you work remotely*, we joked, though of course we were wrong.

It quickly became apparent that I was sheltered: good communication and compassion were built into the support function. On Engineering, as the men wrote high-minded manifestos about the importance of collaboration, everyone else struggled to get their contributions reviewed and accepted. Some men shipped huge parts of the platform based on internal popularity, while women's code was picked apart or dismissed. The company promoted equality and openness, until it came to stock grants: equity packages described as nonnegotiable were, in fact, negotiable for those who were used to successfully negotiating. The infamous name-your-own-salary policy had resulted in a pay gap so severe that a number of women had recently received corrective increases of close to forty thousand dollars. No back pay.

Over the next few days, I wandered the bowels of the city's

convention center, where eight thousand students and technology professionals had gathered in a semi-coordinated attempt to capture each other's attention. There were booths for all the large technology corporations, and for startups from every investment-firm fiefdom. Temporary stalls draped in cheap dark fabric had been erected along the sidelines, inside of which corporate recruiters conducted job interviews. I found it reassuring to see companies focused on biotech, robotics, health care, renewable energy—staid and serious organizations that did not reflect the startup giddiness of consumer tech to which I had grown accustomed in San Francisco.

Among the computer science majors, I felt vaguely out of place, then embarrassed to have impostor syndrome at a conference designed to empower women in the workforce. I made sure to keep my identification badge, which prominently displayed the logo of the open-source startup, over my T-shirt, which prominently displayed the logo of the open-source startup. I stood behind the booth and handed out stickers of the octopus-cat costumed as Rosie the Riveter, the Statue of Liberty, a Día de los Muertos skeleton, and a female engineer—swooshy bangs, ponytail, cartoon hoodie decorated with the octopus-cat.

As I watched a flood of young women pass out their résumés and chat about careers they hadn't started yet, I felt heartened, inspired. Perhaps I will work for you one day, I thought, feeling expansive and corny. I wished, vaguely, that I had stuck with the programming exercises the previous year. My skill set had never exactly been on the cutting edge of technology, not even close, but I already felt myself sliding toward obsolescence. There was the sense that my coworkers and I were coming face-to-face with our replacements, and I envied the younger women's futures. I also felt, in a maternal way, responsible for them.

Everyone I knew in tech had a story, first- or secondhand. That week, I heard new ones: the woman who had been offered an engineering job, only to see the offer revoked when she tried to negotiate a higher salary; the woman who had been told, to her face, that she was not a culture fit. The woman demoted after maternity leave. The woman who had been raped by a "10X" engineer, then pushed out of the company after reporting to HR. The woman who had been slipped GHB by a friend of her CEO. We had all been told, at some point or another, that diversity initiatives were discriminatory against white men; that there were more men in engineering because men were innately more talented. Women kept personal incident logs. They kept spreadsheets. They kept tabs. Some were beginning to step forward and speak about their experiences openly. It felt like the start of a sea change.

Not everyone was excited by the public conversation. Some prominent founders and investors, habituated to fatuous coverage of playful workplaces and unfiltered, idealistic CEOs, did not appreciate this style of media attention. They blamed journalists who reported on sexual harassment for making the industry look bad; they claimed the media were jealous because the tech industry was eating their lunch. They complained that complaints about the boys' club discouraged girls from pursuing STEM, as if this were all just a matter of marketing. Some women, would-be scabs, chimed in to say that they'd had male mentors, and were just fine. The level of discourse could use a boost.

During the conference's keynote speech, the CEO of a highly litigious Seattle-based software conglomerate encouraged women to refrain from asking for raises. "It's not really about asking for the raise, but knowing and having faith that the system will give you the right raises as you go along," he said. "That might be one of the additional superpowers that, quite frankly, women who don't ask for raises have." Better, he offered, to trust karma.

At a Male Allies Plenary Panel, a group of women engineers circulated hundreds of handmade bingo boards among attendees. Inside each square was a different indictment: *Mentions his mother. Says "That would never happen in my company." Wearables. Asserts another male executive's heart is in the right place. Says feminist activism scares women away from tech.* At the center of the board was a square that just said *Pipeline.* I had heard the pipeline argument, that there simply weren't enough women and underrepresented minorities in STEM fields to fill open roles. Having been privy to the hiring process, I found it incredibly suspect.

What's the wearable thing, I asked an engineer sitting in my row. "Oh, you know," she said, waving dismissively toward the stage, with its rainbow-lit scrim. "Smart bras. Tech jewelry. They're the only kind of hardware these guys can imagine women caring about." What would a smart bra even do? I wondered, touching the band of my dumb underwire.

The male allies, all trim, white executives, took their seats and began offering wisdom on how to manage workplace discrimination. "The best thing you can do is excel," said a VP at the search-engine giant whose well-publicized hobby was stratosphere jumping. "Just push through whatever boundaries you see in front of you, and be great."

Don't get discouraged, another implored—just keep working hard. Throughout the theater, pencils scratched.

"Speak up, and be confident," said a third. "Speak up, and be heard."

Engineers tended to complexify things, the stratosphere jumper said—like pipelines.

A woman in the audience slapped her pencil down. "Bingo!" she called out.

The open-source startup was still coming out of crisis mode. It was as if someone had switched the lights on at a party, and everyone was scrambling to tidy up, looking around for paper towels and trash bags, rubbing red eyes and scrounging for mints. Installing Human Resources and promoting employees with no managerial experience to middle-management roles with no authority. Rolling up the "In Meritocracy We Trust" flags. Removing "stay classy" from the job listings. Striking the culture-fit interview. Disabling the prompt, /metronome, that dropped an animated GIF of a pendulous cock into the all-company chat room. Hiring bartenders to enforce a drink limit. Wondering what else might be broken, and how quickly it could be fixed.

Call it crisis management, corporate responsibility, or catching up to the zeitgeist: the open-source startup decided to become an industry leader in the "diversity space." The CEO hired a management consultant, a bubbly and no-bullshit Latina woman who had graduated from a top business school after attending a renowned private university in Palo Alto that was largely considered a feeder for the tech industry. The consultant's undergraduate class, in the early 1990s, was infamous for having produced a group of entrepreneurs, venture capitalists, and libertarians who had jump-started the internet economy, become dynastically wealthy by their thirties, and given back to society by reinvesting in the ecosystem. The consultant's firsthand familiarity with this milieu—and her knowledge of who, from their cohort, had not accessed such fortune— suggested to me that it was not a coincidence she had dedicated her career to the Sisyphean task of proving to people in positions of power that discrimination in tech not only existed, but should, and could, be addressed.

At HQ, we assembled in small groups in the Rat Pack room for unconscious-bias trainings and roundtable discussions. The conference room could have served as a soundstage for a show about 1960s advertising executives, if not for the flat-screen mounted at one end, on which a grid of employees, disembodied in London and Tokyo and South Carolina, bobbled and glitched. We sat around the heavy wood table, swiveling in orange bucket chairs, and talked about microaggressions, intersectionality, and the cultural values embedded in code. I eyed the silver bar cart and the elegant midcentury credenza, and wondered whether it might also be worth spending some time on the cultural values embedded in interior design.

The consultant knew her audience. She pitched diversity to us as if it were enterprise software. Many companies treated diversity as window dressing, she said: diversity and inclusion were used as a PR play, a nice-to-have, which often manifested as a siloed office on the Human Resources floor that occasionally proffered tax-deductible gifts to uncontroversial nonprofit organizations. But diversity, the consultant explained, wasn't just about doing the right thing. We needed to see diversity as a business asset, and as central to the value proposition. It was critical for innovation and needed to be treated as such, at every level of the company.

Most of my coworkers were excited about the diversity and inclusion initiatives. Like the majority of tech workers I knew, they were open-minded, smart, and receptive to new ideas— though for some of them, the discussion was hardly novel, only overdue. That the company was starting to take them seriously was hugely gratifying.

There was a smaller subset, however, for whom viewing

power through an intersectional lens was a new way of looking at the world, one they were being told was not only the new normal in their workplace, but a morally correct position. They asked whether, by focusing on diversity, the company was lowering the bar. Just asking questions, they said: What about diversity of experience? What about diversity of thought? Tech had a lot of Asians and Asian-Americans, they pointed out—maybe not in leadership roles, but still, shouldn't that count for something? They argued about the pipeline problem. They argued about genetic predisposition. They argued that tech wasn't perfect, but at least it was more open-minded than other industries, like finance. They internalized the critique of meritocracy as a critique of open-source. The consultant listened patiently as my colleagues microaggressed her.

"Meritocracy": a word that had originated in social satire and was adopted in sincerity by an industry that could be its own best caricature. It was the operating philosophy for companies that flirted with administering IQ tests to prospective and existing employees; for startups full of men who looked strikingly similar to the CEO; for investors undisturbed by the allocation of 96 percent of venture capital to men; for billionaires who still believed they were underdogs because their wealth was bound up in equity.

I understood why the idea appealed, especially at a time of great economic insecurity, and especially for a generation that had come of age around the financial collapse. Nobody was guaranteed any future, I knew. But for those who seemed to be emerging from the wreckage victorious—namely, those of us who had secured a place in an industry that had steamrolled its way to relevance—the meritocracy narrative was a cover for lack of structural analysis. It smoothed things out. It was flattering, and exculpatory, and painful for some people to part with.

The consultant assembled a task force of employees, a sort of internal focus group, and called it a diversity council. I applied to join; my desire to be a teacher's pet was so deeply ingrained, it was basically pathological. Once a week, twenty of us sat around a conference table and discussed the startup's problems. We complained. We divulged. We processed. A woman who built internal tools recommended that the men read *Feminism Is for Everybody*, and they solemnly nodded. It all felt like intellectually engaged, important work. I couldn't believe I was getting paid to do it.

Late one morning, on the way to HQ, I spotted a middle-aged man in the light-rail station wearing one of the octopus-cat hoodies. He was sitting upright on a piece of cardboard, a bent paper cup beside him, and was not wearing shoes. On his ankle was an open wound. Below us, I could see a train, maybe mine, pulling in. I rushed through the turnstile, wondering if I should have given him money, then wondering if I only felt that way because of the octopus-cat. I found a seat on the train and pressed my head against the window like a child.

The train emerged aboveground and onto the Embarcadero, curving past a gigantic pop-art sculpture of a bow and arrow. The bay glittered and lapped, seagulls descended on a neglected bakery bag, and I felt disturbed. The man seemed like a novelistic apparition, a hallucination.

When I got into the office, I described to a coworker how surreal it had been, like whiplash. It was the city's socioeconomic gap personified, I said. It felt even more significant that the man in the light-rail station was black, and not just because San Francisco was losing its black population at a rapid clip. To my knowledge, our company had just two black employees.

Just so on the nose, I said. My coworker nodded. "That is really sad," he said. We stood there, as if observing a moment of silence. "I wonder whose it was," he said. "We're not supposed to give away the hoodies."

I knew, even as I was moving through them, that I would look back on my late twenties as a period when I was lucky to live in one of the most beautiful cities in the country, unburdened by debt, untethered from a workplace, obligated to zero dependents, in love, freer and healthier and with more potential than ever before and anytime thereafter—and spent almost all my waking hours with my neck bent at an unnatural angle, staring into a computer. And I knew, even then, that I would regret it.

I had reached the promised land for millennial knowledge work. I was making eighty, ninety, then a hundred thousand dollars a year doing a job that only existed for, and on, the internet. Mostly, I wrote emails for a living. Mostly, I worked from home. The job asked so little of me, I might have forgotten I had it—except for the fact that it required me to be online.

Some days, clocking in to work was like entering a tunnel. I would drop a waving-hand emoji into the team chat room, answer a round of customer tickets, read email, process a few copyright takedowns, and skim the internal message boards: work-anniversary posts written by colleagues to thank their bosses and commemorate themselves (*humbled and grateful to learn and grow*); product-release notes (*proud to ship our team's newest feature*); baby announcements formatted as product-release notes (*proud to ship our team's newest feature*). In the chat software, I moved from channel to channel, reading information and banter that had accumulated overnight in other time zones. After repeating this cycle, I would open a new browser window and begin the day's true work: toggling between tabs.

The browser was sick with user-generated opinions and misinformation. I was in a million places at once. My mind pooled with strangers' ideas, each joke or observation or damning polemic as distracting and ephemeral as the next.

It wasn't just me. Everyone I knew was stuck in a feedback loop with themselves. Technology companies stood by, ready to become everyone's library, memory, personality. I read whatever the other nodes in my social networks were reading. I listened to whatever music the algorithm told me to. Wherever I traveled on the internet, I saw my own data reflected back at me: if a jade face-roller stalked me from news site to news site, I was reminded of my red skin and passive vanity. If the personalized playlists were full of sad singer-songwriters, I could only blame myself for getting the algorithm depressed.

My New York friends were hanging out without me, the algorithms showed, and people I'd never met were hanging out without me, too. Everyone was working on their personal mythologies. B-list actors and celebrity fitness instructors were getting centered in Iceland. Beautiful women in wide-legged canvas pants were doing beautiful things: making candy and throwing pots, wallpapering apartments with hand-painted patterns, drizzling yogurt over everything, eating breakfast salads.

The algorithm told me what my aesthetic was: the same as everyone else I knew.

The platforms, designed to accommodate and harvest infinite data, inspired an infinite scroll. They encouraged a cultural impulse to fill all spare time with someone else's thoughts. The internet was a collective howl, an outlet for everyone to prove that they mattered. The full spectrum of human emotion infused social platforms. Grief, joy, anxiety, mundanity flowed. People were saying nothing, and saying it all the time. Strangers swapped confidences with other strangers in return for unaccredited psychological advice. They shared stories of private infidelities and public incontinence; photos of their bedroom interiors; photos, faded and cherished, of long-dead family members; photos of their miscarriages. People were giving themselves away at every opportunity.

Information and temporality collided. Amber alerts hovered above neighborhood notices about package theft and raccoons in the recycling. Animated GIFs of nineties rappers slid above ASMR videos; corporate recognitions of terrorist attacks and school shootings were smashed between in-depth discussions of reality television and viral recipes for chicken thighs. Accounts representing national organizations defending civil liberties campaigned for human-rights issues on top of indie musicians vying for sponsorship from anthropomorphized denim brands. Everything was simultaneously happening in real time and preserved for posterity, in perpetuity.

Often, I would catch myself examining a stranger's acai bowl; or watching frantic videos of abdominal routines that I lacked the core muscles to imitate; or zooming in on a photograph of a wine cellar in Aspen; or watching an aerial video of hands assembling a tiny, intricate bowl of udon noodle soup,

and wonder what I was doing with myself. My brain had become a trash vortex, representations upon representations. Then
again, I hadn't known what a wine cellar was supposed to look
like.

I careened across the internet like a drunk, tabbing: small-
space decoration ideas; author interviews; videos of cake frost-
ing; Renaissance paintings with feminist captions. Cats eating
lemons. Ducks eating peas. Rube Goldberg machines, *Soul
Train* episodes, 1970s tennis matches, Borscht Belt comedy.
Stadium concerts from before I was born. Marriage proposals
and post-deployment reunions and gender reveals: moments
of bracing intimacy between people I did not know, and never
would.

A stranger in the heartland held a tabby cat up to her bathroom
mirror. The tabby sagged. "Say hi," the woman said.

"Hi," said the cat.

A stranger danced on a stripper pole with a baby riding
her calf.

A stranger's disembodied hands slowly shaved soap.

A stranger got married in a castle in Nice.

A stranger did a set of kettlebell swings using a woman as a
weight, while a dog licked itself on the couch.

I searched for answers, excuses, context, conclusions: *Define: tech-
nocracy. California ideology. Jeffersonian democracy. Electronic
agora. Ebola. State slogans. New dark mole. Tanuki. Feminist porn.
Feminist porn not annoying. What is canned ham? How old too
old law school? Best law schools. Law schools rolling admissions.*

Islamic State. Silk pajamas. Elbow moisturizer. Unshrink wool sweater. What is mukbang. Define: pathos. Define: superstructure. "Jobless recovery." White noise Arctic ice cracking. Cuba tourism. How to massage your own shoulder. Text neck. Vitamin D deficiency. Homemade silverfish trap. Rent calculator. The Big One when. Hypnosis nail biting. Hong Kong protests. Dishwasher video inside. Ferguson indictment. Satellite images of my parents' childhood homes. The names of my ex-boyfriends' bands. The time I could expect the sun to set that evening.

I found myself watching videos of antiwar protests from the sixties; videos of antiwar protests I had marched in as a teen. Videos detailing conspiracy theories about a missing commercial plane. Videos I wouldn't even know to search for: *The rain forest hermit who stepped out of the wild. Twins get mystifying DNA results. Baby gender reveal!! (Dance). Funniest unboxing fails and hilarious moments 3. Geek wizardry magic trick. My Son Was a School Shooter: This is My Story. How to Do a Body Slam.*

Sometimes I would worry about my internet habits and force myself away from the computer, to read a magazine or a book. Contemporary literature offered no respite: I would find prose cluttered with data points, tenuous historical connections, detail so finely tuned it could only have been extracted from a feverish night of search-engine queries. Aphorisms were in; authors were wired. I would pick up books that had been heavily documented on social media, only to find that the books themselves had a curatorial affect: beautiful descriptions of little substance, arranged in elegant vignettes—gestural text, the equivalent of a rumpled linen bedsheet or a bunch of dahlias placed just so.

Oh, I would think, turning the page. This author is addicted to the internet, too.

•

Just me and my id, hanging out, clicking.

Customer ticket after customer ticket: like swatting flies.

I refreshed the newspaper. I refreshed social media. I refreshed the heavily moderated message board. I scrolled and scrolled and scrolled.

In any case. Time passed, inevitably and unmemorably, in this manner.

O ne slow evening, working from a couch at HQ, my laptop chimed with an instant message from the CEO of the analytics startup. I felt a jolt of dread: we did not text. I reminded myself that I no longer worked for him. I owed him nothing. I did not have to reply, now or ever.

Hi! I replied immediately.

The CEO told me he had a proposition. I instinctively picked up my laptop and moved into the lactation room, which had recently been labeled with a plaque: WORD TO YOUR MOTHER'S ROOM. I felt ridiculous—who was I hiding from? My manager lived in Amsterdam. Nobody was looking at my computer. I was not lactating. But the chair was plush. The room was dark and warm.

The analytics startup was spinning up a marketing team, the CEO wrote. Did I want to come back and do content? I'd been interested in it before, he noted, and I knew the product well. *I thought I'd see if perhaps you were still in love with the idea*, he wrote.

Love, I thought. Negged again.

I thought about my coworkers on the other side of the door, congregating after yoga class and eating tubes of popped wild rice. When I had absconded to the lactation room, a developer was sitting shoeless on one of the couches, playing an unplugged electric guitar. It was practically idyllic, except that I had hardly spoken to anyone in person all day.

We're bigger now. It's a different place, the CEO added. Then: *Not super-different.* I appreciated this hedge. I thanked him, and told him I would think it over.

"Last time you did content, they didn't want to pay you for it," Ian reminded me that night, when I told him about the offer. "You have nothing to prove. Are you really considering this?"

Not seriously, I lied.

I had chosen to leave, I said, but I still felt pushed out of the club. It could be nice to overwrite my own feelings of failure, on my own terms: to prove to the CEO, and to myself, that I belonged. Ian squinted at me. "I don't think your stubbornness about this will ever be rewarded," he said. "If you want to write, write about something you care about, not about stuff like how to use funnels for user onboarding."

It could be a good chance to own something, I said, unconvincingly; I couldn't imagine the CEO ever letting an employee own anything. I could build out a portfolio, I said. It could be interesting.

We exchanged a meaningful look. "Not that interesting," Ian said.

I went to New York. On previous trips home, when I was still working at the analytics startup, the city had felt fraught with paths not taken. All these past selves, marching around like they knew something; casting aspersions on my all-encompassing tech-centric identity; trying to convince me I had made a mistake. This time, I felt lighter. I reported into work from my childhood bedroom, making myself available between six in the morning and early afternoon. I saw college friends, and didn't try to recruit anyone. I drank coffee with my mother until the coffee ran out or ran cold; visited my grandparents in apartments that hadn't changed for decades. I tried to clear out the storage space in the basement, unearthing old bomber jackets with hand-sewn patches, undergraduate writing, a jar of peeled potatoes stockpiled fifteen years prior in preparation for Y2K. Banal activities, but they felt so good. I felt myself returning to myself.

It was strange to be back, but with tech money. I invited friends to dinner at restaurants I knew about from my boss at the literary agency, opened bar tabs, took cabs home after midnight instead of waiting for the train. Killing time in an over air conditioned wine bar in the West Village one evening, sucking on Castelvetrano olives and feeling fancy, I thought about a conversation I'd once had with Noah, in which he had described joining the tech industry as both a personal defeat and a concession to his hometown's new identity. Money, he said, gave him access to San Francisco's growing network of private spaces, which had become most of the city. Money was a key.

New York held my whole life, but the city I had grown up in no longer existed. There were some holdouts—the cat-smelling bookstore where I had worked during college breaks, certain cultural institutions—but the neighborhoods I had known as a child were now dotted with restaurants playing overdetermined playlists and boutiques trading on a branded locality that I found comical and alienating. The new version of the city was inscrutable, baffling. Who wanted this? Who was it for?

In North Brooklyn, I asked a bookseller about the new buildings on the waterfront. The bookstore was full of over-sized art books that were easy to imagine sitting on glass-top coffee tables in glass-walled apartments. I couldn't find any-thing I wanted to read. Who lives there, I asked. The bookseller shrugged, and straightened a display of unlined notebooks. "Wall Street people, hedge fund types," he said. "Tech bros." Tech bros, I thought—here, too.

The nature of cities was to change, I knew. I tried not to feel entitled: I was aware that my parents, who had moved to Brooklyn in the early 1980s, had once been the outsiders re-writing the borough, just as I had spent four years contributing to the erosion of Polish and Puerto Rican Greenpoint. I knew that I was doing the same thing out west, no matter how many times I tried to tell myself that it was temporary. Acceptance of complicity, on both coasts, was still a passive act. It ameliorated nothing.

The city was beginning to look like a generic idea, per-haps sprung from the mind of a real estate developer, of what a wealthy metropolis should be. Developers could make condos out of anything. Young money ran amok. There were so many coworking spaces and upscale salad shops; so many anemic new buildings with narrow balconies. Walking through downtown Brooklyn, the force of time tumbling forward, I felt, for a moment, that I might viscerally understand some of the rage and grief I witnessed from longtime residents back in San Francisco.

Toward the end of the trip, I went with my friend Leah to see a performance by a musician and choreographer we both knew. The show was beautiful and strange, unsettling. Watching dancers roll gently across the floor of the black-box theater, I cried a little, wiping my nose on the program. I felt moved, buoyant, more alive, and desperately impressed with our friend—for making art in the face of a culture that hardly valued creative work, for building a life around it, for his grace and conviction. I glanced at Leah, a check on my passions; she held her chin in her hands, significantly more dignified but no less transfixed.

The performance had a two-night run. It may have been video-recorded, but it felt like it was just for us. Afterward, the choreographer stood in the theater lobby, flushed and bashful, receiving bouquets wrapped in butcher paper. People in structurally inventive clothing lingered to synthesize over plastic cups of wine. We kissed the choreographer and gave our congratulations, then shuffled over to let in friends waiting on the periphery.

As we left the theater in pursuit of a hamburger, I felt rising frustration and resentment. I was frustrated because I felt stuck, and I was resentful because I was stuck in an industry that was chipping away at so many things I cared about. I did not want to be an ingrate, but I had trouble seeing why writing support emails for a venture-funded startup should offer more economic stability and reward than creative work or civic contributions. None of this was new information—and it was not as if tech had disrupted a golden age of well-compensated artists—but I felt it fresh. I emitted this stream of consciousness at Leah, swearing to delete my ad-blockers and music apps, while she hailed us a cab.

"Why not just leave, find something else you're excited about?" she asked, as we rumbled across the Williamsburg Bridge, heading toward the restaurant where she worked.

Money and health insurance, I said—and the lifestyle. I

had never really considered myself someone with a lifestyle, but of course I was, and insofar as I was aware of one now, I liked it. The tech industry was making me a perfect consumer of the world it was creating. It wasn't just about leisure, the easy access to nice food and private transportation and abundant personal entertainment. It was the work culture, too: what Silicon Valley got right, how it felt to be there. The energy of being surrounded by people who so easily articulated, and satisfied, their desires. The feeling that everything was just within reach.

Was I trying too hard to make this mean something? I asked Leah. Was that just buying into the industry's own narratives about itself? I tried to summarize the frantic, self-important work culture in Silicon Valley, how everyone was optimizing their bodies for longer lives, which could then be spent productively; how it was frowned upon to acknowledge that a tech job was a transaction rather than a noble mission or a seat on a rocket ship. In this respect, it was not unlike book publishing: talking about doing work for money felt like screaming the safe word. While perhaps not unique to tech—it may even have been endemic to a generation—the expectation was overbearing.

Why did it feel so taboo, I asked, to approach work the way most people did, as a trade of my time and labor for money? Why did we have to pretend it was all so fun?

Leah nodded, curls bobbing. "That's real," she said. "But I wonder if you're forcing things. Your job can be in service of the rest of your life." She reached out to squeeze my wrist, then leaned her head against the window. "You're allowed to enjoy your life," she said. The city streaked past, the bridge cables flickering like a delay, or a glitch.

•

At the airport a week later, waiting to board my return flight, a man standing at the front of the line caught my eye. He looked familiar, in a distant-relative, someone's-husband sort of way. I shuffled closer, overstuffed camping backpack digging into my shoulders, and realized it was the CEO of the e-book startup. Standing beside him were the CPO and CTO. Even in the terminal's fluorescence, all three looked trim and energized. Their carry-on bags were modest in size and immaculate. I had wolfed a turkey sandwich in the food court, and was aware that I had a slight mustard odor. I already felt disarmed by their good attitudes.

The founders and I greeted each other warmly. I was a little surprised that they remembered me—over two years had passed, a decade in startup time. I was ancient history. The e-book startup had grown, raising an additional seventeen million dollars and expanding to include women and an editorial staff. The company even had an online literary magazine, which I tried not to take personally. I wondered if the founders had actually liked me. I wondered if they were seated in business class.

"Where are you these days?" asked the CEO, with characteristic enthusiasm. I felt bad that I hadn't followed up, and worse that I couldn't tell him I had launched my own company or at least become a junior analyst at a venture firm. I said I was working at the open-source startup, and the founders seemed to approve; then I added that I was doing customer support, and watched their faces shift to a polite neutral. I've also started writing book reviews, I appended meekly. I had written a handful of reviews for a magazine my mother once described fondly as "the ideological left talking to itself" but that was now being driven into the ground by its new owner, a billionaire cofounder of the social network everyone hated. I knew the founders would be familiar with the billionaire owner; it seemed less likely they read the magazine. They nodded supportively.

The men were vague about their plans for the Bay Area. Just some meetings, they said. I asked if they might have free time, and they clarified that it would be a quick visit. Right, I thought, business. What did I think we were going to do, go on another field trip? I was delusional. After a few minutes I said goodbye, and returned to my boarding group at the back of the line.

A few months later, reading the heavily moderated message board, I better understood their vagueness: the e-book startup was closing the service. They had probably been in San Francisco to meet with their investors, wind things down. The company had been purchased by the search-engine giant, in what was rumored to be an eight-figure acquihire.

Back in San Francisco, I felt acutely aware of the city's beauty, and of the inbound aesthetic shift. Half the knowledge workers I encountered had the same thin cashmere sweaters I did, and the same lightweight eyeglasses. Some of us had the same skin tints, from the same foundation. We complained of the same back problems, induced by the same memory-foam mattresses. In apartments decorated with the same furniture and painted the same shades of security-deposit white, we placed the same ceramic planters holding the same low-maintenance plants.

Efficiency, the central value of software, was the consumer innovation of a generation. Silicon Valley might have promoted a style of individualism, but scale bred homogeneity. Venture-funded, online-only, direct-to-consumer retailers had hired chatty copywriters to speak to the affluent and overextended, and we appeared to be listening.

The direct-to-consumer companies sold cotton T-shirts, toothbrushes, rubber trees, rash cream, skin cream, leather bags, meal replacements, luggage, linens, contact lenses, cookies, hair dye, athleisure, wristwatches, vitamins. On any given night in America, exhausted parents and New Year's–resolution cooks were unpacking identical cardboard boxes shipped by meal-prep startups, disposing of identical piles of plastic packaging, and sitting down to identical dishes. Homogeneity was a small price to pay for the erasure of decision fatigue. It liberated our minds to pursue other endeavors, like work.

Persuaded by the testimonials of two infrastructure engineers, overnight converts to orthotic sensibility, I ordered a pair of unembellished, monochrome merino-wool sneakers. I'd been noticing them on people in coffee shops and in line at no-cash food trucks, and in advertisements on my social media feeds. The sneakers looked like a child's drawing of a shoe, a shoe distilled to its essence, but they were incredibly comfortable. I didn't know if wearing them outside was an act of radical self-respect, or the exact opposite. They sat unworn by the apartment door, a monument to the end of sensuousness.

Wasting time on the microblogging platform one morning, I fell into an argument with the founder of a startup who was making the case, to his seventy thousand followers, that books should be shorter and more efficient. *It's unfortunate that the world doesn't reward conciseness more*, he posted. *Making books shorter would effectively increase the rate at which we can learn. Or, put another way, the broken incentives today are probably *halving* (or more) the rate at which you can learn. Be mad!*

I was mad. Mad that tech entrepreneurs like him seemed constitutionally unable to resist cannibalizing music, books, subcultures—whatever made life interesting. Reading wasn't about mainlining information. The tech industry's efficiency fetish was so dreary. Don't encourage your claque, I thought. I took a screenshot of his post, and shared it with a little editorialization: *Tech needs to stop trying to ruin everything I love*, I sniped.

My social media use usually tapped out at making jokes about books with a small group of friends, but the post began to circulate, and I began to panic. I wasn't used to having an audience, and didn't want one. It was preferable to lurk, ideal to be invisible. Also: didn't I have anything better to do?

I clicked through to the founder's profile page. *Optimist, fallibilist*, read the account bio. *CEO*. The avatar was a professional headshot. His shoulders curved forward, clavicle protruding from the neck of a loose cotton T-shirt. The only other people I knew with professional photographs were aspiring actors who needed to audition for Hollywood films and antacid commercials, but he could have been cast: he was handsome, and had an air of self-possession. I could practically hear the photographer advising him to soften his eyes, to look focused but compassionate.

Optimist in which way, I wondered. In the *Candide* way, the Jeffersonian way, or the Oscar Wilde way? I looked up *Oscar Wilde optimism quote*—"The basis of optimism is sheer terror"—and felt affirmed. I looked up "fallibilist" and found myself on a website about philosophy and medieval mathematical truths.

When I searched the optimistic, fallibilistic CEO's name, the search engine autofilled the appendages "girlfriend" and "net worth." On social media, he posted earnestly about biographies of physicists and tech luminaries, and shared sweeping landscape photographs from trail runs and bike rides. He was younger than I was, but that was starting to seem like a given.

As I was about to close out the search results, I saw a photograph of him as a teenager, dressed in a Catholic school uniform. His tie was tucked into his sweater, and he brandished a trophy from a prestigious science competition, a look of sheepish pride stretched across his face. He could have been any one of my friends from high school. It was impossible not to smile back at my laptop.

I followed up, though the CEO had not responded, and

added an apology, tagging him into the conversation I was having with myself. He quickly wrote back, and the disagreement migrated over to email, where he invited me for lunch.

A few weeks later, I biked from work to his company's office in the Mission. With teenage-like impudence and a vain savior complex—I had the ear of a social media influencer, I thought, and not only would I bend it, I would introduce it to *art*—I had brought along a small stack of books to give him, all of which espoused different versions of my own aesthetic or political inclinations. They also pandered to what I believed were his interests, in that they were short. At the top of the pile was a copy of *Are Prisons Obsolete?*, about which I was especially smug. I cruised through SoMa, congratulating myself on speaking truth to power, sticking it to the Man.

The CEO met me at reception, and introduced himself as Patrick. He was skinny and freckled, with glacier eyes and a mop of curls—much less intimidating than the headshot, much more polite than the Man. He wore running sneakers and a lightweight athletic jacket. We walked to a café and sat on a bench outside, eating lentil salad and rehashing our conversation from the microblogging platform.

To my surprise, I liked him. He was wry, and very charming. He spoke in complete, eloquent paragraphs. We compared notes on working at pickax companies and the books we were reading, and swapped childhood stories. He told me about studying ancient Greek with a monk in the countryside where he grew up, and the drifting, lost time he'd spent between his first startup and the current one. Later, I would hear him repeat these same anecdotes in media interviews and feel a little cheated: I wasn't used to people with well-worn origin stories. Then again, I wasn't used to being around people who were asked for them.

I told Patrick about my book reviewing, and he asked whether it was something I wanted to do full-time. Oh, I said— that's not a job. I made a joke about the golden handcuffs of startup health insurance, and he asked if health insurance was the one thing keeping me from quitting my job and pursuing my goals. No, I said, worried that he might offer to pay for it. The one thing keeping me from pursuing my goals was that I didn't know what, exactly, my goals were.

"Ah," he said, pushing a lentil around the biodegradable container. There were qualities I wanted for my professional life, I continued, quickly. I wanted work to be intellectually engaging, and I wanted to do it alongside smart, curious people. I wanted long-term projects. I wanted it to matter. Patrick listened patiently as I processed fourteen years of liberal arts education and aspirational upper-middle-class messaging in real time. Then we sat quietly for a moment, gazing into the street, my directionlessness like a third wheel.

We walked back to my bike. As we stood by the door to his office, I handed Patrick *Are Prisons Obsolete?*, and he grew animated. He was fascinated with the American prison-industrial complex, he said. Incarceration in the United States was one of the greatest shames of the modern era. History would indict us, he said, and history would be right. Knowing he had dropped out of college, I offered to share the syllabus from a seminar I'd taken on the carceral state. He politely sipped the dregs of his iced tea.

As employees filtered past, the energy shifted. I was reminded of the gulf between us: Patrick was running a company, and I processed copyright takedowns and held users' hands through account lockouts. I'd trolled him on the internet, and he'd taken the time to buy me lunch. He was the picture of grace, and I was lowly, unfocused, a rando with no goals. I wondered what kind of boss he was.

We shook hands again, as if at the end of a job interview, and agreed to be in touch. It seemed safe to assume I would never see him again. Still, I had so many questions, so many things I wanted to talk to him about. A prison abolitionist who knew ancient Greek did not fit neatly into the archetype of a tech founder. I biked uphill toward my apartment, past tent encampments and antique streetcars, against the fog.

The message-board commentariat argued about whether it was more rewarding to work hard or work smart. They quantified qualitative things in amazing ways. *Simple math*, posted a data scientist at a company I'd never heard of. *Monday to Friday is 71% of the week. The job won't get done with 71% effort.* I read the men's disagreements while lying naked in bed with my work-issued laptop, keeping one eye on the queue.

People argued about whether burnout was real, but also about burnout's economic rewards. They shared links to pop-science articles about the creative potential of procrastination. They admired China's "996" work schedule: 9:00 a.m. to 9:00 p.m., six days a week. They considered the value of seeing their young children; certain formative years were more important to be around for than others, some said.

The men debated the role of equity in the ecosystem, the incentives for making fuck-you money. *It's about independence*, one of the men wrote. *It's about the freedom to take a personal risk.* When I thought risk, I didn't think about money, mine or anyone else's. Risk was white jeans on my period, coffee on an airplane, hitchhiking, the pull-out method. But the men weren't talking to, or about, me; they never were. *It's about leverage*, posted a self-described top performer. *It lets me grab our executives and board by the balls.*

Fuck-you money: it was a catchphrase, a motivation, a life-style. According to people on the internet taking a dip in the shallow pools of libertarianism, it was pure American freedom. It was a state of mind, argued a startup founder on his company blog—it was an attitude. Money: it wasn't about the money. After a certain threshold, at least, it really wasn't.

A venture capitalist who would later be the subject of sex-ual harassment allegations helpfully chimed in to say that fuck-you money went much further in Thailand. By his metrics, a million dollars in Southeast Asia would be more than enough. *Maybe even a few hundred thou*, he wrote.

Side arguments broke out about whether financial gain— the prospect of fuck-you money, that luscious carrot on the stick—was the right incentive for startup employees. *I disagree with the premise*, wrote a man whose handle invoked an imagi-nary animal. *Are you implying that the only reason to work is for the money?*

I did see Patrick again. We met for dinner at a restaurant on the far side of Bernal Hill, an outgrowth of another internet ar-gument; then dinner in the Mission, an outgrowth of an unfin-ished conversation; then dinner in the Outer Sunset, at which point we had established a friendship that felt nearly familial in its combativeness and ease.

Patrick complicated my expectations for the entrepreneurial class. He did not exhibit much desire to strut across confer-ence stages or digitally thought-lead; it was impossible to imag-ine him bullying employees or doing shots. Friends who met him often assumed he was a graduate student. We had little in common, in terms of our extracurricular interests—one eve-ning, walking past a DIY venue, he looked at the art-punk kids standing outside and said, dryly, "So this is where the youth go for the bippity boppity"—but I found this very relaxing. No pretenses; no posturing. He wore thin-framed glasses that improved his vision without signaling any subcultural affiliation, and was wildly smart. I always wanted to know his opinion.

We mostly spent time together in upscale New American restaurants, where Patrick had no trouble making same-day reservations. The restaurants were full of natural fibers and acacia accents, unobtrusive flora and barre-body waitresses in linen shifts; couples in their thirties and forties, the women wearing sturdy ankle boots and understated engagement rings, the men dressed, typically, to traverse a glacier. There was always at least one table of startup employees out for a team-building dinner, tucked somewhere they would not overly influence the ambience.

San Francisco was going through a culinary renaissance, a competitive effort to capture the attention of young money. Chefs were not competing with each other so much as against the apathy inspired by upscale office cafeterias, fast casual, and delivery apps. To differentiate themselves, they spun the dial all the way up, treating fried anchovies like luxury items and meting out slices of sourdough bread like manna from heaven. The food was demented: cheese courses hidden beneath table candles and revealed, perfectly softened, at the end of the meal; whole quail baked into loaves of bread. It was high-intensity, sensory overload: smoked corn-husk chawanmushi, pickled French fries, green beans and cherries enrobed in burrata. Food that the chef mandated be eaten by hand. Food that was social media famous. Food that wanted to be.

After a string of starched-linen dinners, the friendship started to feel a little formal. We attempted alternate activities: a hike

at six in the morning, a power breakfast at seven. Finally, I realized dinner was just the way Patrick hung out; it was the only
consistent block of personal time in his schedule.

It was easy to interrogate everyone's relationship to power
and status except for my own. I did not really care that Patrick ran a company, but I knew that other people did. I was
flattered that he wanted to be friends with me, and surprised
that he put in the time and the work. This brought out a side
of my personality I wasn't proud of. I let him off the hook for
things I would have called out in other friends: he was not
a reliable communicator, he could be curt, he would solicit
time-consuming input on various projects and forget to acknowledge the feedback. When he interviewed a close friend
of mine for a job, only to go dark, I felt ashamed, and annoyed,
and said nothing. But Patrick had calls to take, meetings to
run, time zones to juggle, flights to catch, teams to manage,
executives to hire, investors to please. His time was no more
valuable than my time, his life no more important than anyone else's life—except, by the terms governing the ecosystem,
it was.

Walking through the Mission to meet Ian for dinner, I bumped
into one of the support engineers from the analytics startup.
"My army buddy," he said, embracing me. He smelled like mango
vape. I laughed, not realizing he was serious. "We've been in the
shit together," he continued. "I've held you in my arms while
you cried your heart out, like the world was ending." I adored
him, but I did not remember crying into anyone's arms—I had
always been careful to cry alone, in the bathroom. I was certain
this had not happened. I said so, and he shrugged. "Why would
you remember it?" he asked. "It was a totally normal thing to

happen in that environment." I did not tell him that I had recently considered returning.

We stood on the street, hands in our pockets, stepping out of the way for commuters and shoppers and a woman pushing a cart of personal possessions. The support engineer told me that he had left the company. The CTO, the wide-eyed, self-taught genius, had left, too.

"I heard he sold a bunch of his stock back," the support engineer continued. "Instant multimillionaire. No question." There was a question, actually: we had no way of knowing whether he'd sold his stock back and made millions. Still, the story seemed plausible enough. It was thrilling to even consider that the dream had come alive for someone we knew, of whom we were fond. Though the CTO had had a managerial title, I had always considered him one of us.

What do you think he wants to do next? I asked. I wondered if the CTO might be working on his own games. I was excited for him.

The support engineer thought about it a moment. "Good question," he said. "I don't think he wants to do anything."

I joined a new team, Terms of Service, created to deal with the overflow of semi-legal concerns and complaints about objectionable material that choked the support queue. The open-source platform was, at its core, a file-hosting service: users could upload text, images, animations, and documents. While the interface could be intimidating to people who were not programmers, the public product was still used and abused like any other social technology that relied on free, user-generated content.

The Terms of Service team handled copyright takedowns, trademark infringement, and spam; user deaths and COPPA violations. We took over the work of the Hazmat group, evaluating threats of violence, cryptocurrency scams, phishing sites, suicide notes, and conspiracy theories. We puzzled over reports of Great Firewall circumvention. We ran emails claiming to be from the Russian government through translation software and passed them to Legal with spinning question-mark emojis. We sifted through reports of harassment, revenge porn, child porn, and terrorist content. We pinged our more technical coworkers to examine malware and purportedly malicious scripts.

We became reluctant content moderators, and realized we needed content policies. My teammates were thoughtful and clever, opinionated but fair. Speaking for a platform, however, was nearly impossible, and none of us were particularly well qualified to do it. We wanted to tread lightly: core participants in the open-source software community were sensitive to corporate oversight, and we didn't want to undercut anyone's techno-utopianism by becoming an overreaching arm of the company-state.

We wanted to be on the side of human rights, free speech and free expression, creativity and equality. At the same time, it was an international platform, and who among us could have articulated a coherent stance on international human rights? We sat in our apartments tapping on laptops purchased from a consumer-hardware company that touted workplace tenets of diversity and liberalism but manufactured its products in exploitative Chinese factories using copper and cobalt mined in Congo by children. We were all from North America. We were all white, and in our twenties and thirties. These were not individual moral failings, but they didn't help. We were aware we had blind spots. They were still blind spots.

We struggled to draw the lines. We tried to distinguish between a political act and a political view; between praise of violent people and praise of violence; between commentary and intention. We tried to decipher trolls' tactical irony. We made mistakes.

Coming to decisions was, of course, as complex and nuanced and subject to interpretation as the content itself. Even pornography was a gray zone: nipples needed to be contextualized, but we weren't trying to be puritanical. An artistic photograph of a woman breastfeeding was not the same as an avatar of an anime character spouting milk from physiologically untenable breasts. But what was art, anyway, and who were we to define it?

Intent mattered, we reminded each other—repositories that contained assets for sex-education websites, for example, should be acceptable. At the same time, the platform was meant to be educational. We didn't necessarily want people looking for package managers stumbling across folders of genitalia instead.

I sometimes wondered whether the executive team knew that there was pornography or neo-Nazi drivel on the platform, or that well-intentioned employees working under Support, people who had been hired for intangible qualities like "good judgment" and "attention to detail," were constantly bugging Legal to define—and enforce—what would be understood as the company's position on free speech.

Most of the company did not seem aware of how common it was for our tools to be abused. They did not even seem to know that our team existed. It wasn't their fault—we were easy to miss. There were four of us for the platform's nine million users.

The list of chat channels was growing: *Latinx*, *Neurodiverse*, *40+*, *Octoprentices*, *Octoqueer*, *NB*, *Blacktocats*. The diversity and inclusion consultant had come on full-time, as VP of a new team called Social Impact, and with her guidance the startup was slowly becoming more diverse. Activists joined, as did some of the startup's most vocal critics.

One of these critics, Danilo, could have been a poster child for meritocracy—he was born to a single mother in Puerto Rico, raised in public housing, and had taught himself how to code as a kid—but he spoke openly about his contempt for Silicon Valley's rugged-individualist narratives, and was fond of mocking venture capitalists and rabid techno-libertarians on social media. He clearly made some of our coworkers nervous.

Danilo's vision for technology was new to me. It relied on disruption, as was the fashion, but what it disrupted was Silicon Valley. The cost of participation in technology was plummeting, he liked to point out. As education, hardware, and access to tools got cheaper, more people would participate. The products and companies would diversify; the power structure would morph. "A whole new generation of technologists will do an end run around our whole system," he told me, as we worked together one afternoon from HQ, sitting onstage in the empty event space. "We have this space with unprecedented influence and leverage for social change, and a whole generation coming up that was raised on broadband. That generation is going to come in and fuck it up." Even venture capitalists would eventually be disrupted and rendered obsolete. I found this all very exciting—a way to reformat cynicism about the industry as optimism about the future.

In late fall, the VP of Social Impact arranged for a visit from the secretary of Housing and Urban Development. The company had been working on an initiative of his, to bridge the digital divide by bringing high-speed internet, computers, and educational programs to people in low-income housing. I had spent a week in Washington, D.C., sitting in on meetings about the initiative, and had found it encouraging to hear elected officials—rather than the industry's self-appointed leaders of borderless digital societies—talk about how technology could change the world.

The day of the secretary's visit, the office buzzed. The CEO posted to the internal message board, alerting us to the presence of actual Secret Service. Members of the Social Impact team looked anxious, electrified, as a phalanx of publicists and mixed-tier security toured the secretary through HQ. The actual Secret Service's elegant suits and pins, in sober comparison to our Secret Service's octopus-cat shirts, made me wince.

Did they walk him through the Oval Office? I asked a coworker. She closed her eyes. "We are so fucking embarrassing," she said.

At the designated hour, everyone filed into the third-floor amphitheater. We came off a little careless and irreverent, I thought, surveying the loose T-shirts and scuffed-up shoes my colleagues and I were wearing. Various midlevel managers rushed around, instructing employees on where to sit. I hadn't seen so many people in the office since our holiday party.

Danilo gave a brief introduction. "The internet is an accelerant for growth and a dissolver of class walls," he said. "It is a global classroom and community." Out of the corner of my eye, I saw one of the company's lawyers eating a miniature candy bar and looking peacefully stoned.

"Most of all, it is the ticket to twenty-first-century prosperity," he continued. "As a technologist, I feel a moral duty to help ensure its gifts reach all who need them." I heard the rustle of polypropylene and the snap of a crispy peanut-butter core. The lawyer stared straight ahead, chewing.

The secretary and the VP of Social Impact discussed the initiative. A quarter of United States households did not own a home computer, they noted; the digital literacy gap was also a gap in opportunity. The secretary, wearing a full suit and gleaming leather brogues, looked polished and hyperrealistic in the way that politicians tend to look. He looked out of place. I wondered what it felt like to lead a life of public service—climbing the ladder, accumulating credentials, walking the thinnest lines, probably owning a tuxedo—only to find himself catering to the growing power center of Silicon Valley, with its baby tyrants, all the one-hit wonders who had dropped out of school and become their own bosses and thought they knew how the world worked, thought they knew how to fix everything. All the unicorn companies with in-house lobbyists poached from political consultancies, the billionaires who resisted regulation and expertise. Maybe it felt the same as catering to Wall Street, or the pharmaceutical industry, or Big Agriculture. Maybe it felt like envy: tech, after all, was a foil for some of the bureaucratic tedium that addled government. Anyone who had been to the DMV could make a case for disruption. Then again, I could only imagine the nightmare that would be a startup-run regulatory body.

At the end of the presentations, our CEO, in low-riding jeans and a blazer, reemerged for closing remarks. He strode across the stage with an employee sweatshirt draped over his arm, just like the ones worn by our locally famous engineers. He and the secretary of HUD shook hands. As a token of thanks, the CEO said, he was proud to present the secretary with his very own personalized hoodie.

On the train to HQ one morning, scrolling through social media apps on my phone, an algorithm served up a photograph taken at the analytics startup's holiday party. The photograph was of two former coworkers, both of them smiling broadly, their teeth as white as I remembered. "So grateful to be part of such an amazing team," the caption read. The party had its own hashtag, and I tapped through.

The hashtag unleashed a stream of photographs featuring people I'd never met—beautiful people, the kind of people who looked good in athleisure. They looked well rested. They looked relaxed and happy. They looked nothing like me.

I swiped to a photograph of what could only be the pre-dinner floor show: an acrobat in a leotard kneeling on a pedestal, her legs contorted, her feet grasping a bow and arrow, poised to release. Her target was a stuffed heart, printed with the company logo. I scrolled past animated photo-booth GIFs of strangers kissing and mugging for the camera, and I recognized their pride, I empathized with their sense of accomplishment—it had been one hell of a year, but they had made it, and they had won. I felt gently ill, a callback to the childhood nausea of being left out.

I kept scrolling until I landed on a video of the after-party, which looked like it had been filmed in a club or at an expensive bar mitzvah, save for the startup's logo projected onto the wall. Flashing colored lights illuminated men in disassembled suits and women in cocktail dresses, all of them bouncing up and down, waving glow sticks and lightsabers to a background of electronic dance music. They've gone pro, I thought. The company had recently raised an additional sixty-five million dollars. They had a war chest. They were bound for hypergrowth. They were sparing no expense.

Last night was epic! read a comment from someone I'd never met. Over a year had passed since I left. I caught myself searching for my own face anyway.

At the beginning of the new year, Ian's robotics studio moved down to Mountain View, to merge with the search-engine giant's clandestine research-and-development facility. The facility, housed in what had once been California's first indoor mall, was called the moonshot factory. Straight-faced, immodest. Employees were asked to use the phrase on their email signatures and professional résumés; their director went by Captain of Moonshots. I still didn't know what Ian actually worked on, although sometimes I learned from the news: papers of record had reporters covering the search-engine giant as a dedicated beat, like a foreign government, a new kind of nation.

From time to time, the company also distributed T-shirts printed with internal code names—further clues. What is "Hi-Lo"? I asked, when Ian showed up wearing a company shirt that looked like it had come from a prog-rock concert. He couldn't say. I told him this was deeply annoying: if things were at the promotional T-shirt phase, employees should be able to talk about their work. "Well, sure," he said. "But isn't that part of the fun?"

The company was fun. It was fun—it was fun!—and it wanted

everyone, especially employees and prospective employees, to know. Engineers zipped across the mall on bikes and scooters. The Captain of Moonshots was always on Rollerblades, gliding between commitments, reducing inefficiency and boosting his heart rate. Ian attended a picnic with a quadruped military robot, as if a mule-sized piece of metal that could open doors by itself were a normal dining companion. The company threw a Día de los Muertos party, with Mexican food, a mariachi band, and a candlelit altar that paid tribute to products killed before launch. It hosted a multiday off-site at a former Boy Scout camp in the redwoods—a heavy-handed metaphor, I thought.

The search-engine giant offered perks that landed somewhere between the collegiate and the feudal. Ian got check-ups at the health center and returned home with condoms the color of the company's logo, printed with the words I'M FEELING LUCKY. Employees were offered a roster of physical-education opportunities—not just Rollerblading—and Ian started attending intensive functional fitness classes during his lunch hour. He began lifting, bulking, quantifying; I began finding protein bar wrappers in the lint trap. "I'm worried I'm becoming a brogrammer," he said, pulling up an app to show me his stats. I was not worried about Ian becoming a brogrammer—I was more concerned about him seeing his colleagues naked in the communal locker room. It all seemed so intimate. He reassured me that it was a big company.

The parent corporation, which employed some seventy thousand people, was a world-historical summit of engineering talent—a limitless resource to explore, an organizational marvel—but it looked, from the outside, like it was suffering from a certain degree of sclerosis. It was the best big company to work for, Ian sometimes said, but the core business was still digital advertising, not hardware.

As executives shuffled and reshuffled the acquisitions, it began to seem as if the moonshot factory had vacuumed up some of the more innovative companies in robotics, then put them on the back burner for several years. Later, we would read in the news about a number of sexual harassment charges against the men Ian referred to as his super-bosses. These offered at least a few useful explanations for institutional stagnancy. The super-bosses must have been busy.

The round-trip commute to Mountain View could take up to four hours. The evening time that Ian had once spent biking the city, or cooking dinner with friends, or rolling around on the floor in the new-age ballet class we took together, he now spent on the corporate shuttle. In the mornings, Ian sprinted to the pickup point, thermos of coffee in hand. In the evenings, the bus ejected him back into the fog. I could see him from the bay window as he trudged down the block looking enervated, queasy, and gray.

I sometimes wondered whether there was a unique psychic burden shared by people who worked in technology, specifically those of us building and supporting software that existed only in the cloud. The abstractions of knowledge work were well documented, but this felt new. It was not just the cognitive dissonance of how lucrative and powerful tech companies had become, when their tools did not physically exist, but that all software was vulnerable, at any time, to erasure. Engineers could spend years writing programs only to have them updated, rewritten, and replaced. They poured hours and energy into products that never shipped. Offensive as it was, I wondered if the Día de los Muertos party had provided some closure for the people whose work never went live.

My own psychic burden was that I could command a six-figure salary, yet I did not know how to do anything. Whatever I learned to do in my late twenties, I learned from online tutorials: how to remove mold from a windowsill; slow-cook fish; straighten a cowlick; self-administer a breast exam. Whenever I wrenched a piece of self-assembly furniture into place, or reinforced a loose button, I experienced an unfamiliar and antiquated type of satisfaction. I went so far as to buy a sewing machine, like I was looking for ways to shame myself.

I wasn't alone. Half the programmers I knew between the ages of twenty-two and forty, mostly men, were discovering that their fingers were multipurpose. "It feels so good to do something with my hands," they said, before launching into monologues about woodworking or home-brewing or baking sourdough. It was like Brooklyn five years ago, except instead of pickling vegetables, the hobbyist artisans examined each other's crumb shots. At work, a handful of the engineers became obsessed with sous vide, and on weekends they seared, sliced, and plated soft meat, documenting their process and sharing proud, high-resolution pictures on social media.

I envied Ian, who was trained to think in terms of hardware, the embodied world. He stared at a computer all day, too, but the laws of physics still applied. His relationship to the internet was different from mine: he didn't have accounts on any of the social networks, was unfamiliar with memes and unattuned to the minutiae of other people's lives. He didn't stand up at the end of the day and think, as I did: Oh, right—a body.

I left my apartment to meet Patrick for dinner at a restaurant with a cinema theme. Talk quickly turned to tech, per usual; per usual, I began projecting my anxieties and frustrations about

Silicon Valley onto him. Our disagreements about the industry were ongoing, like a podcast no one in their right mind would listen to. The same information could bring us to radically different conclusions—what I interpreted as a cautionary tale, he might read as a blueprint, and vice versa—but I enjoyed these conversations. They expanded the frame and sharpened the edges of my own arguments. Only occasionally did I stalk home in the dark, listening to loud music and feeling grim, wishing I worked in another sector or lived in another city—namely, one where I could bum a cigarette.

"Would I prefer a counterfactual Silicon Valley that only produced meaningful companies?" he asked, as we were presented with matching plates of fried chicken slathered in yogurt and dukkah. "Of course. But I think the genomic startups and the bullshit startups are the outcome of the same process, the foibles and the self-destructive tendencies, all that. If we could have sane, judicious, sober, prudent, well-adjusted Silicon Valley, producing the same companies, that would be great, but I'm not sure we can."

Of course we can, I said. Most startups would probably be just as successful, if not more so, if they were run by people who did not, for example, harass or ostracize the women in their engineering organizations. They would probably be just as innovative, run by people who weren't—no offense—young, white, and male. And how were we defining success here, anyway? I asked, getting a little excited, though I was the one who had brought up success in the first place. Shouldn't more and different kinds of people be allowed to fail? I sipped on my wine, feeling triumphant.

"To be clear, I agree with the critiques," Patrick said, refilling my water glass suggestively. "I also want Silicon Valley to be better. More inclusive, more ambitious, more significant, more serious. More optimistic." On this we agreed, though I suspected we might have different ideas about how it could manifest. "I think it's really striking that there is only one Silicon Valley, and I worry a lot about that flame being extinguished. Maybe one question is whether you would want two Silicon Valleys, or none. For me, that answer is really clear."

I swirled a piece of chicken skin around my plate. I did not want two Silicon Valleys. I was starting to think the one we already had was doing enough damage. Or, maybe I did want two, but only if the second one was completely different, an evil twin: Matriarchal Silicon Valley. Separatist-feminist Silicon Valley. Small-scale, well-researched, slow-motion, regulated Silicon Valley—men could hold leadership roles in that one, but only if they never used the word "blitzscale" or referred to business as war. I knew my ideas were contradictions in terms.

"Progress is so unusual and so rare, and we're all out hunting, trying to find El Dorado," Patrick said. "Almost everyone's going to return empty-handed. Sober, responsible adults aren't going to quit their jobs and lives to build companies that, in the end, may not even be worth it. It requires, in a visceral way, a sort of self-sacrificing." Only later did I consider that he might have been trying to tell me something.

Friends hosted a rave in the Sacramento Delta, billed as a radical self-reliance event. *The land is dry and needs your sweat*, read the invitation. *We are itching to fill the farm with joyful, hungry bodies*. I wanted to be a joyful body—or, at least, I wanted to try. To prepare, I packed a pair of black harem pants, a small vaporizer, a novel, and *The Artist's Way*. "I don't think people read at raves," Ian said, eyeing my tote bag, but he let it go.

When we pulled up to the farmhouse, a group of shirtless men were erecting a geodesic dome. They laced strings of LEDs around the poles, their pectorals tensing, and propped pillows and futon mattresses around the interior. In an outdoor kitchen, people chopped toppings for pizza. A lamb skittered between their legs, looking for scraps. Portable speakers played electro swing.

The party's host was a communitarian farmer with an easygoing, searching personality. As the farmer helped us set up our tent in a walnut grove, I asked what the story was with the lamb. The plan, he said, snaking a pole through the fly, was to spit-roast her the next afternoon. "You wrestle her to the ground and spoon her until she relaxes," he explained, as if he were sharing a recipe for fruit salad. "Then you just reach around and slit her throat."

In the late afternoon, a man and woman emerged from the woods, dressed in white, loose linen. They announced that there would be a ritual. They were regal in face paint, pink from the sun. Everyone lined up, passing a joint from front to back, and marched down to the creek, where they disrobed. Our leaders, still partially clothed, waded into the water and took turns dipping everyone backward, like a baptism. The linen floated to the surface like scum. No way, I whispered to Ian. Too goyish. I hung back and kept my suit on, joining once the ritual was over.

The naked bodies bobbed downstream. They clambered up to the edge of the creek and communed with the livestock on the other side, and lay out to dry in the drooping sun. Cans of beer floated in the creek. I felt a familiar loneliness, participating in something bigger than myself and still feeling apart from it.

After a while, I climbed out of the water, feeling self-conscious. I shook out a towel next to Ian and an acquaintance who made money cuddling with older men. The cuddle therapist sat cross-legged, his testicles draped with great trust over a small patch of wildflowers. I insinuated myself into Ian's armpit. We inquired about his sessions: How did it feel to be the object of so much yearning? Did people cry, or confess? Was it heavy; did it feel like an important service? What happened if someone got aroused? "If you get a boner, you have to get up," the cuddle therapist said, with infinite patience. Ian idly detangled my hair.

Even on the farm, people were talking startups. With a measure of reluctance outdone only by the exhaustion of precarity,

Noah and Ian's friends had begun moving into the industry; the ecosystem found a way to absorb those with college degrees and fluency in middle-class social cues. A principal at a public elementary school took a job at an education startup making scheduling software. A music critic wrote copy about fitness and meditation apps. Journalists switched into corporate communications. Artists took residencies at the social network everyone hated, and filmmakers found themselves in-house at the larger tech corporations, shooting internal promotional content designed to make workers feel good about their professional affiliations.

Everyone needed a hustle: artists, musicians, blue-collar workers, and public servants were leaving San Francisco, and new ones were not taking their place. In blond-wood coffee shops that opened for people who wanted to take meetings in coffee shops, the baristas were not, as they had once been, young and new to the city. They were older and softer and still protected, at least for the moment, by rent control, but the writing was on the wall. Even comedians began offering corporate improv seminars, workshops for startup employees to strengthen team relationships through mutual humiliation. "What's your opinion on coding boot camps?" the cuddle therapist asked Ian.

That evening, in the orchard, a group of musicians who had been touring the West Coast in a retrofitted school bus performed songs about California. The sky grew dark. Black widow spiders were discovered in one of the portable toilets, setting off a displacement initiative. Five or six people disappeared to have sex in a walk-in refrigerator. Others took ketamine and danced slowly to house music, or reclined on faux-fur blankets in the geodesic dome, doing poppers. A woman wearing a sequined tutu took PCP and perched on a heap of firewood. "There's just so much to look at," she said, saucer-eyed, bursting with awe.

Sometimes it felt as if everyone had watched a highlight reel of people enacting freedom in the sixties and seventies—casual nudism, gleeful promiscuity, communal living, communal eating, communal bathing. There had been some talk of buying group land up near Mendocino. There had been some talk of shared childcare, even though no one had children. It struck me as a performance from an imperfect past, a reenactment. The pursuit of liberation, some pure joy.

I did not see myself becoming an executor of the sixties counterculture, but I was interested in its endurance—even startup founders held company retreats at Sea Ranch. Everywhere else, the counterculture was a historical subject, a costume-party theme, kitsch. Certainly, this side of the sixties was not a reference for my friends in New York. They had back-to-the-land fantasies, too, of a sort: renovated barns up the Hudson, with vegetable gardens and vintage pickup trucks and farmhouse sinks. Utopianism did not loom large. I didn't know if this indicated clear-eyed realism or a failure of imagination.

Around midnight, I returned alone to the tent and zipped myself into a sleeping bag, Ian's fleece camping pillow bundled under my head. I wondered if all this was perhaps just a form of resistance. Technology was gnawing into relationships, community, identity, the commons. Maybe nostalgia was just an instinctual response to the sense that materiality was disappearing from the world. I wanted to find my own way to hedge against it, my own form of collective.

Beneath me, the earth was hard and cold. It vibrated, perpetually, to the bass line.

From time to time, friends from outside the industry would post articles about psychological experiments run by the social network everyone hated, with their own baffled commentary, to the social network everyone hated. They would email me news stories about facial-recognition software, or a ride-sharing startup's ability to track riders with a tool called God View. *Did you know about this?* they would write. *Is this . . . normal?* They would text, suspicious or amused, after stumbling into corners of the internet that spooked them: the microblogging platform served ads for groceries they had just purchased, or a photo-sharing app recommended connecting with a long-lost acquaintance they had just seen on the subway. Food delivery services would suggest local restaurants during far-flung vacations; voice assistants would blurt information unprompted.

"Check this out," a friend said over drinks, passing his phone across the table to show me a log of his most frequent locations: home, his office, the gym, train stations, an unknown residential address I didn't ask about. "My phone has been building a little dossier on my behavior, like a private eye. I don't know whether to feel flattered or deceived."

When I failed to demonstrate surprise, or tried to explain what was happening, or even admitted that some of this was actually related to the work I had done at the analytics startup, my friends' reactions made me feel like a sociopath. These conversations didn't make me feel superior or culturally knowledgeable. They scared me. I would hang up the phone and wonder whether the NSA whistleblower had been the first moral test for my generation of entrepreneurs and tech workers, and we had blown it. I would look across the table into the confused faces of smart, hopeful, well-informed participants in civil society, and think, with dismay: They really don't know.

At work, corners of the open-source platform were growing increasingly vicious and bizarre. The Terms of Service team was alerted to content posted by people claiming to be members of a terrorist organization; content posted by people who were doxing government employees and stalking our coworkers. We were alerted to content that contained targeted death threats. One was credible enough to shutter HQ for a day.

We debated what to do about code for a game in which players competed to kill Jews. We squinted at repositories full of ASCII art that spelled out phrases like *FAGGOTS ARE GAY BUT NOT QUEERS* and *VAPE IN MY PUSSY AND CALL ME YOUR MEME SLUT.* We passed around account avatars of iconic cartoon animals styled to look like Hitler, and responded in the chat room with shrugging emojis styled to look like us.

Most days, I stuck to processing copyright takedowns and

trademark reports, following tedious procedures with great satisfaction, like a proud paralegal for the open-source community.
Other days, I sent polite emails to users asking them to please
change out the swastikas they were using for their avatars, or to
consider removing the anti-Semitic comics they had uploaded
to their repositories.

I often had to step back and remember that this sort of
material accounted for a minuscule fraction of activity on the
open-source platform. In the grand scheme of things, the company was lucky: unlike the traditional social networks, it did
not offer a way to livestream graphic acts of violence. Unlike
the home-sharing platform and car-hailing apps, it was not in
the business of in-person interactions. By comparison, the tool
facilitated a very specific, benign form of digital civic life. No
one was signing in to form an opinion about abortion or the cur-
vature of the earth; no one was looking to be debriefed on the
news. The majority of users engaged with the site as intended.

Still, I had long since stopped doing public work under my
own name. For all external correspondence, I used male pseudonyms. Thankfully, we never had to use the phone. I did this
in part because the work could be sensitive, with the potential
to upset people whose digital currency was cruelty; I wasn't the
only person on the team using a fake name. But using male
pseudonyms wasn't just useful for defusing or de-escalating
tense exchanges. It was useful for even the most harmless
support requests. I was most effective when I removed myself.
Men, I saw, simply responded differently to men. My male
pseudonyms had more authority than I did.

It was still the era of the social web. Everyone in the pool.
Alone, together. Social networks, claimed the social networks'

founders, were tools for connection and the free circulation of information. Social would build communities and break down barriers. Pay no attention to that ad tech behind the curtain: social would make people kinder, fairer, more empathetic. Social was a public utility for a global economy that was rapidly becoming borderless, unbounded—or would be, if anyone in Silicon Valley could figure out how to win China.

Social would bring liberal democracy to the world. Social would redistribute power and set people free, and users would determine their own destinies. Deeply rooted authoritarian governments were no match for design thinking and PHP applications. The founders pointed to Cairo. They pointed to Moscow. They pointed to Tunisia. They side-eyed Zuccotti Park.

Not that the platforms themselves betrayed revolutionary potential—they looked innocuous, because they looked the same. Stiff, flat, gray, blue. Hard-edged, but trying hard to be friendly. Built by programmers with programmers in mind, for and by people with a penchant for infrastructure. People accustomed to looking at tabular data, for whom coding was creative, and good code was clean. People who thought that personalization was the responsibility of an algorithm. Systems thinkers, for whom the system was computational, and did not extend into the realm of the social.

The software was transactional, fast, scalable, diffuse. Crowdfunding requests for insulin spread as quickly and efficiently as anti-vaccination propaganda. Abuses were considered edge cases, on the margin—flaws that could be corrected by spam filters, or content moderators, or self-regulation by unpaid community members. No one wanted to admit that abuses were structurally inevitable: indicators that the systems—optimized for stickiness and amplification, endless engagement—were not only healthy, but working exactly as designed.

•

In the spring, a far-right publication ran a blog post about the VP of Social Impact, zeroing in on her critique of diversity-in-tech initiatives that tended to disproportionately benefit white women. The post ran with a collage of octopus-cats, under the headline ANTI-WHITE AGENDA REVEALED.

The article sparked a furor in the comments section, accumulating hundreds of responses. The publication's readers made conspiratorial statements about Marxism and Hollywood, liberal victimhood, reverse racism, and the globalist agenda. They published panicked micro-essays about the Federalist Papers and North Venezuela, and the cultural extermination of the West. It was a cacophony of dog whistles.

The comments section burst. Menacing vitriol about my coworkers spread across social media. The Sales line rang with rabid callers. The publication seemed to have mobilized a faction that was hell-bent on amplifying far-right ideas under the guise of political debate, using any available channel. By the end of the day, the VP, the CEO, and a handful of outspoken employees had become targets of a vicious internet harassment campaign. It was not the first time this had happened to coworkers—it was, to my knowledge, already the third instance in a year.

The campaign was a barrage; it persisted for days. Some of the threats were specific enough that the company hired security escorts. HQ had an uneasy air. A threatening note was found taped to the door of the employee entrance.

I mentioned to a coworker how striking it was that all internet harassment now seemed to follow a playbook: the methods of the far-right commentariat were remarkably similar to what we had seen, eighteen months prior, from the troll bloc targeting women in gaming. It was like an entire generation had developed its political identity online, using the style and tone of internet forums.

Is this just how things are now? I asked. It was bizarre to me that two different groups would have the same rhetorical and tactical strategies.

My coworker was a connoisseur of online forums and bulletin boards. He looked at me askance. "Oh, my sweet summer child," he said. "They are absolutely the same people."

Silicon Valley had become a gesture, an idea, an expansion, and an erasure. A shorthand and a Rorschach test. A dream or a mirage. There was confusion over whether the South Bay was a bedroom community for San Francisco, or the converse. Both appeared to be true.

Tech was only about 10 percent of the workforce, but it had an outsized impact. The city was turning over. People kept coming. The Mission was plastered with flyers addressing newcomers. *Nobody cares about your tech job*, the flyers read. *Be courteous of others when in public and keep the feral careerism of your collegial banter on mute.*

Rents rose. Cafés went cashless. The roads were choked with ride-shares. Taquerias shuttered and reopened as upscale, organic taco shops. Tenement buildings burned, and were replaced with empty condominiums.

On the side of San Francisco where streets were named after union organizers and Mexican anti-imperialists, speculators snapped up vinyl-sided starter homes and flipped them.

Amid tidy rows of pastel Edwardians, the flipped houses looked like dead teeth, muted and ominous in freshly painted, staid shades of gray. Newly flush twentysomethings became meek, baby-faced landlords, apologetically invoking arcane housing law to evict inherited long-term tenants and clear the way for condo conversions. Real estate developers planned blocks of micro-apartments, insistent that they weren't just weekend crash pads, but the new frontier of millennial living: start small, scale up later.

Against the former factories and chipping Victorians, the car-repair shops and leather bars, downtown's new developments looked placeless, adrift. To differentiate themselves, they added electronic locks and Wi-Fi-enabled refrigerators, and called the apartments smart. They offered bocce courts, climbing walls, pools, cooking classes, concierge services. Some hosted ski trips to Tahoe and weekend trips to wine country. They boasted bicycle lockers, woodworking shops, dog-wash stations, electric-car chargers. Half had tech rooms and coworking lounges: business centers designed to look like the residents' offices, which were themselves designed to look like home.

Outside my studio, a pickup truck backed into the tea tree, killing it. The tree was removed and replaced with a portable toilet identical to the portable toilet across the street. Neither was for use by the neighborhood's growing population of homeless people, some of whom were left to defecate in succulent planters and in the shadows of garage overhangs, but for the construction crews that arrived every morning to build out junior one-bedrooms in the basements of facing Victorians. This was a landlord's market.

The toilets were both padlocked, and routinely broken into. At night, I lay in bed at the base of the bay window, listening to people struggle with the shackle; the sound of the plastic door swinging open, shuddering shut.

Glossy photographs of well-coiffed real estate agents began appearing in my mailbox, printed on card stock with calligraphic fonts. The agents were excited to unveil a gorgeous oasis with soaking tub and matte cabinetry; they were delighted to share an adorable bungalow with original details and breakfast nook. The agents pitched proximity to the freeways, and inserted maps of the tech shuttle routes, color-coded by company. *Coveted location*, the brochures read. *Fabulous investment property with no rent control.* I stood on the steps of my apartment building, looking at the agents' headshots and thinking about bleaching my teeth.

San Francisco had tipped into a full-blown housing crisis. Whenever the media reported that a new tech company had filed an S-1 with the SEC, people started comparing notes on tenants' rights. Buy a house before the next IPO, my coworkers joked. It wasn't a joke because it was funny; it was a joke because the overnight-wealthy were bidding 60 percent over asking on million-dollar starter homes, and paying in cash.

Four of the six apartments in my rent-controlled building were occupied by middle-aged couples, some of whom had been there since at least the last boom; they were familiar with the rhetoric of community and revolution, had heard it all before. The recent flood of euphoric young people in pursuit of professional adventure, and the flood of cash that followed, was stressful, not impressive. I suspected no one in our building was in the market for a passive-income property, or a million-dollar condo. I suspected they all just wanted to stay.

The real estate brochures came hard and fast. They began

to address the building's owner, who did not live there, and offered enticements to flip. *Hi neighbor!* they chirped. *I wanted to share the big news about recently sold homes in your area.*

We have considered and ready buyers eager to invest in your neighborhood.

If you could get the right price for your home, would you sell?

The brochures collected on top of the mailboxes like a come-on and a taunt—reminders of our luck, and our impermanence.

There was a lot of discussion that year, particularly among the entrepreneurial class, about city-building. Everyone was reading *The Power Broker*—or, at least, reading summaries. Everyone was reading *Season of the Witch*. Armchair urbanists blogged about Jane Jacobs and discovered Haussmann, Le Corbusier. They fantasized about charter cities. They were beginning to notice something interesting—a potential opportunity, perhaps—taking place outside the windows of their ride-shares. They were beginning to catch on to the value of civic life.

At a party, I met a man who leaned in and told me, with warm breath, that he was trying to get involved with an exciting new urbanism project. His T-shirt was creased geometrically, as if he'd had it same-day delivered and only unfolded it an hour ago: artful dishevelment in the age of on-demand. I asked if he worked for the city, or in urban planning. He'd gotten his start like the rest of us, he said, gesturing vaguely around the room, which was full of technologists. But he'd been meaning to read more about urbanism, if I had any book recommendations.

I thought about the college syllabi from my undergraduate courses in urban studies and felt a flash of superiority, but couldn't remember any of the titles. I inquired about the project, and he hesitated, the pause of someone drunk enough to be itchy with a secret, but not so drunk he wanted to make mistakes. I waited.

Cities were important, he began, as if warming up for a pitch; as if we did not tacitly agree on this, standing in a living room in a famous urban center. "But cities could be smarter," he said. "They should be smarter. What if we were given a blank slate? What problems could we fix?"

Men were always talking about our problems. Who was the we? "We have all these new technologies at our disposal," he said. "Self-driving cars, predictive analytics, drones. How can we put them together into the perfect combination?" I resisted making a joke about central planning.

I asked where the first blank-slate city would be, expecting him to say somewhere in California—outside of Sacramento, maybe, somewhere within commuting distance that would release some of the pressure from San Francisco.

Central America, he said. Maybe El Salvador. "Somewhere with people who want to work hard, and don't want to have to deal with crime," he explained. I stared, with great interest, at the bottom of my beer bottle. "The idea is to follow lean-startup methodology. The city will start small, like an early startup that has to cater to the first hundred users, rather than the first million." I asked how he planned to scale up, and regretted it as soon as he gave me the answer: shipping containers.

To live in? I asked. What about community? People didn't come from nowhere. What about the local economy? I was starting to get mad. I was starting to show my cards. "Ideally, it would be a special economic zone," he said. "You know Shenzhen?" I knew Shenzhen: a high-gloss, highly surveilled city where rapid economic growth encouraged both luxury development and child-labor abuses; a citizenry partaking of modernity and progress, under dictatorial control. An epiphenomenon of authoritarian capitalism. Did *he* know Shenzhen? I wished I was drunker, so that I could get mean. I asked what the seed round was, intending it as a joke.

They were just bootstrapping, he said. Paying mostly out of pocket—the team was still small. They just needed to raise fifteen million dollars.

City-building was a natural interest for well-capitalized people whose employees could hardly afford to live in the Bay Area and whose corporate patrons and VC hypebeasts instilled the belief that startup founders could not just change the world, but should be the ones to save it. It was a testing ground for the efficacy of a first-principles approach to living.

First-principles thinking: Aristotelian physics, but for the management-science set. Technologists broke down infrastructure and institutions, examined the parts, and redesigned systems their way. College dropouts re-architected the university, skinning it down to online trade schools. Venture capitalists unbundled the subprime mortgage crisis, funding startups offering home loans. Multiple founders raised money to build communal living spaces in neighborhoods where people were getting evicted for living in communal living spaces.

There was a running joke that the tech industry was simply reinventing commodities and services that had long existed. This joke was disliked by many entrepreneurs and venture capitalists, though I thought they should be thankful for the diversion: it moved the conversation away from structural questions about why certain things, like mass transit, or housing, or urban development, had problems in the first place.

On an aesthetic level, I didn't trust the entrepreneurial

class to build a metropolis where most people would want to live. Their impact on San Francisco was not especially inspiring, not that it was entirely their fault. The city was overflowing with new businesses giving new money the hard sell: a store full of minimalist tea kettles; a champagne bar serving caviar on shrimp chips; a members-only coworking clubhouse with boutique exercise classes in a eucalyptus-scented gym. A Ping-Pong club with truffle fries. A shop hawking pencil cases and bento boxes to digital nomads. Gentle-on-the-joints fitness studios: simulated cycling, simulated surfing.

Sometimes, reasoning from first principles was a long and tedious process of returning to the original format. E-commerce sites that hadn't already burned through their venture funding began opening brick-and-mortar flagships—in-person retail, the first-principles approach revealed, was a smart platform for consumer engagement. An online-only glasses retailer found that shoppers appreciated getting their eyes checked; a startup selling luxury stationary bicycles found that luxury cyclists appreciated cycling alongside other people. The mattress purveyors would open showrooms; a makeup startup would open testing counters. The online superstore would open bookstores, the shelves adorned with printed customer reviews and data-driven signage: BOOKS E-READERS FINISH IN 3 DAYS OR LESS. 4.8 STARS AND ABOVE.

There was always something a little off about these spaces— something a little crooked. It was unsettling to find dust on the shelves; strange to see living plants. The stores shared a certain ephemerality, a certain sterility, a certain snap-to-grid style. They seemed to emerge overnight, anchors in physical space: white walls and rounded fonts and bleacher seating, matte simulacra of the world they had replaced.

•

In June, the seed accelerator announced a new initiative. The accelerator was looking to build a new metropolis, entirely from scratch. Jesus, I thought, reading the blog post announcing the initiative. Everyone's getting in on this game. *The world is full of people who aren't realizing their potential in large part because their cities don't provide the opportunities and living conditions necessary for success*, the blog post stated. *A high leverage way to improve our world is to unleash this massive potential by making better cities. Building new cities is the ultimate full-stack startup, in both complexity and ambition.* The post ended with a series of questions: *How should we measure the effectiveness of a city? What are a city's KPIs? What should a city optimize for?*

KPIs, optimization: it reminded me of the analytics software. Who would own the data sets, I wondered; what would they do with them?

The head of the initiative was the former CEO of a website that served as a repository of humorous images and videos optimized for social media virality—mostly cats doing improbable things, like riding robotic vacuum cleaners and getting stuck in hamburger buns. The website had raised nearly forty-two million dollars in venture capital. He would be working alongside another entrepreneur, a woman who had founded an on-demand housekeeping platform that had shut down amid a spate of lawsuits. The audacity was breathtaking.

I wasn't sure why anyone should be so eager to hand the keys to society over to people whose primary qualification was curiosity. I wasn't eager to go to bat for older industries or institutions, but there was something to be said for history, context, deliberation. There was something to be said for expertise. But also, if we *were* going to abandon expertise, I thought, in moments of deep pettiness, then why weren't *my* friends being given millions of dollars to run research projects on making better cities?

What I didn't realize was that technologists' excitement about urbanism wasn't just an enthusiasm for cities, or for building large-scale systems, though these interests were sincere. It was an introductory exercise, a sandbox, a gateway: phase one of settling into newfound political power.

"Do you think you hate yourself?" asked a therapist in Berkeley. Coming on strong for an intake session, I thought, but the next day I caught myself following a bunch of venture capitalists on the microblogging platform. It wasn't exactly an act of self-care.

The venture capitalists were discussing a universal basic income, and I couldn't look away. They were concerned about the unlocked economic potential of the urban poor. As icebergs melted and the ocean's temperatures ticked toward uninhabitability, they were concerned that AI—specifically, the question of whether they or China would own it—would bring about the Third World War. They wanted to see automation and artificial intelligence jump-start a renaissance: the machines would do the work so the rest of us, rendered useless, could focus on our art.

The VCs wanted, one might deduce, to block-grant government services—or, should AI inspire revolution, a rationale for owning bunkers in New Zealand stocked with guns and peanut butter. I'd believe in an AI renaissance as soon as venture capitalists started enrolling in pottery classes; as soon as they were automated out of a job.

The VCs were prolific. They talked like nobody I knew. Sometimes they talked their own book, but most days, they talked Ideas: how to foment enlightenment, how to apply microeconomic theories to complex social problems. The future of media and the decline of higher ed; cultural stagnation and the builder's mind-set. They talked about how to find a good heuristic for generating more ideas, presumably to have more things to talk about.

Despite their feverish advocacy of open markets, deregulation, and continuous innovation, the venture class could not be relied upon for nuanced defenses of capitalism. They sniped about the structural hypocrisy of criticizing capitalism from a smartphone, as if defending capitalism from a smartphone were not grotesque. They saw the world through a kaleidoscope of startups: *If you want to eliminate economic inequality, the most effective way to do it would be to outlaw starting your own company*, wrote the founder of the seed accelerator. *Every vocal anti-capitalist person I've met is a failed entrepreneur*, opined an angel investor. *The SF Bay Area is like Rome or Athens in antiquity*, posted a VC. *Send your best scholars, learn from the masters and meet the other most eminent people in your generation, and then return home with the knowledge and networks you need*. Did they know people could see them?

The venture capitalists were not above inspiration culture. They shared reading lists and product recommendations, and advised their followers to stay humble. Eat healthy, they said; drink less. Travel, meditate, find your why; work on your marriage, never give up. They preached the gospel of eighty-hour workweeks, and talked up the primacy of grit. Whenever they denigrated the idea of work-life balance as soft, or antithetical to the determination necessary for startup success, I wondered how many of them had an executive assistant. A personal assistant. Both.

I couldn't imagine making millions of dollars every year, then choosing to spend my time stirring shit on social media. There was almost a pathos to their internet addiction. Log off, I thought. Just email each other.

Then again, if the internet was good for anything, wasn't it this? Transparency in action; access to the minds of the industry elite. There was no better way to know which venture capitalists wrung their hands over the impact of identity politics on productivity, or how applying Stoic practices to life in Woodside was going. How else to know which members of the venture class defended megalomaniac founders as entrepreneurs who couldn't scale, or mistook criticism as harassment and perceived themselves as victims of digital mobs? How else to understand the deliberately amplified identities, ideologies, and investment strategies of the people transforming society—the people I was helping make rich?

The intellectual culture of Silicon Valley was internet culture: thought-leadership, thought experiments. Message-board intellectualism. There were economists and rationalists; effective altruists, accelerationists, neoprimitivists, millennialists, objectivists, survivalists, archeofuturists, monarchists, futarchists. Neoreactionaries, seasteaders, biohackers, extropians, Bayesians, Hayekians. Tongue-in-cheek and deadly serious. Witting and unwitting. It did leave something to be desired.

At a party in Noe Valley, I fell into an argument with an enthusiastic participant in the online rationality community. Rationalism was considered a truth-seeking movement, at least by its practitioners. In an effort to see the world more clearly, rationalists sampled from behavioral economics, psychology, and decision theory. They talked about argumentation techniques, mental models, and steel men, and deployed the language of science and philosophy: "On balance," they would say, "on margin": "n is net positive"—or "n is net negative," "n is overrated," "n is underrated."

I could get on board with truth-seeking, and as far as I could tell, rationality primarily offered frameworks for living that bordered on self-help. This made sense: religious institutions were eroding, corporations demanded near-spiritual commitments, information overwhelmed, and social connection had been outsourced to the internet—everyone was looking for something.

But rationalism could also be a mode of historical disengagement that ignored or absolved massive power imbalances. A popular rationality podcast covered topics such as free will and moral responsibility; cognitive bias; the ethics of vote trading. When the podcast did an episode with an evolutionary psychologist who identified as a transhumanist, bivalvegan classical liberal, she and the host discussed designer babies optimized for attractiveness without once bringing up race or the history of eugenics. Arguing fervently about a world that was not actually the world struck me as vaguely immoral. At best, it was suspiciously flattering to power. I found the subculture astonishing, not least because it flourished among grown adults.

I had trouble squaring this with the rationalist at the party, who was pleasant and inquisitive. We were sitting at the kitchen island in a scooped-out Edwardian, which had recently been renovated with high-gloss cabinetry and high-gloss walls. The cabinets did not have handles, and everything was white—like a smartphone or a tablet. A group standing around the island had been discussing the venture capitalist who believed software was eating the world, comparing notes on the most valuable insights they had learned from him. I took a pass.

Talk turned to a libertarian economist, an academic and director of a conservative research center. The center was bankrolled by fraternal oil magnates, two right-wing billionaires who had wielded unchecked political influence for decades, but the economist fashioned himself as a contrarian. He blogged on topics such as whether or not price gouging during emergencies could actually be beneficial; whether there was an optimistic explanation for the uptick in racial violence in the United States; whether nations could be startups—African countries looked promising. Perhaps philanthropy was *too* democratic, he posited; perhaps mass conversion of low-income people to Mormonism could lead to greater upward mobility; perhaps we could take a cue from Lagos and consider the constructive capacity of nationalism. His work was popular among the self-styled contrarians of Silicon Valley. I was only aware of him through Patrick, who, to my dismay, was an ardent reader of his blog.

I volunteered that many of the economist's purportedly contrarian opinions—conceived under the guise of being light-hearted thought experiments intended to upend mainstream biases—actually betrayed a much darker vision for society than any of his followers wanted to admit. Most of his ideas were not new; we had simply, as a culture, moved past them already. Was it possible that the libertarian economist was just a reactionary? I said. Just asking questions.

The rationalist swept her hair behind one ear. Contrarianism was underrated, she said. The intellectual contributions were, on net, positive. It was difficult to judge, in the present moment, which ideas would hold water; thus, better to err on the side of more debate, rather than less. "As an example, think of the abolitionists," she said. I asked what the abolitionists had to do with libertarian contrarianism. "Well," she said, "sometimes minority opinions lead to positive and widespread adoption, and are good."

As a neutral statement, this was hard to disagree with. Some minority opinions did lead to positive change. I wanted to give her the benefit of the doubt. But we weren't talking about a neutral statement. We were talking about history.

I took a sip of red wine from a glass that I hoped was mine, and ventured that the abolition of slavery was perhaps not a minority position. Slaves themselves were surely abolitionists, I said. Just because no one was polling them didn't mean they did not exist. I was trying to be lighthearted. I was trying to be kind. I was trying not to embarrass both of us, though that ship might have already sailed.

The rationalist turned to look wistfully at the other party-goers, now gathered in the living room and happily instructing a virtual-assistant speaker to play workout music. She sighed. "Okay," she said. "But, for the sake of argument, what if we limit our sample to white people?"

Venture capital was an intervention, a blunt force. The previous summer, the open-source startup had raised a Series B of two hundred and fifty million dollars, at a valuation of two billion dollars. With the funding came new expectations. The VCs had, after all, doubled down on a business whose foundation was the distribution of free software.

The driving values of venture capital were growth, acceleration, and fast returns, and they could be transformative. They helped explain the search-engine giant's pivot from an academic archive of the world's knowledge into an advertising juggernaut; the proliferation of *ask forgiveness, not permission* and *done is better than perfect* as mantras; the reason "software margins" was practically an aphrodisiac south of San Carlos. Once again, the open-source startup needed to grow up—a little faster this time.

The company had already grown by nearly two hundred people, to five hundred, since I had joined. It was beginning to look a lot like any other company—at least on the surface. There was talk of time sheets, talk of metrics. A spate of experienced corporate players joined the leadership team, and a spate of them left. Leadership was a revolving door. Every few months, Engineering went through a reorganization. No one knew what anyone else was working on; no one knew who was responsible. A high-level executive came on to do strategy; when I asked a coworker what he did, I was told he set strategic meetings.

The board installed a new CFO. Benefits were reevaluated, as were certain job functions. The Oval Office was torn out and replaced by a café, in homage to the startup's decentralized, coffee-shop roots. The café was like every other café—people flirting with the baristas and pretending to work while looking at social media—except the drinks were free. The coder caves were replaced with an open-air workspace. The free swag shop was replaced by a vending machine. Policies were tightened; budgets were slashed. Members of the Social Impact team huddled over cups of tea, looking exhausted and grim. There was convincing evidence we were headed toward an acquisition or exit.

My coworkers and I speculated about who our new parents could be. There were only two real options: the search-engine giant or the highly litigious Seattle-based software conglomerate. The conglomerate had a history of trying to litigate the open-source software community into oblivion, but they had recently shuttered their competitive project, and our founders had not openly gloated.

One of the startup's investors had also posted, to social media, a photograph of the conglomerate's CEO deep in conversation with our CEO at a venture summit. The photograph circulated in private chats and back channels, and we scrutinized it with the obsessiveness of message-board detectives tackling unsolved crimes. "VCs love swinging their dicks at each other," one of my friends in Engineering said. He was convinced we were going to be acquired by the Seattle-based conglomerate. "There's no reason to post that otherwise. I'd be happy, to be honest. I'd probably end up working for one of them anyway."

Salespeople followed capital; they washed in on the tide. They came into the office every day, bringing hypoallergenic designer dogs who got trapped in the elevators and defecated under the desks. They drank cold brew at the bar while flinging around acronyms. They monopolized the third-floor sound system, playing Top 40 and mellow EDM while the engineers migrated to the floors below.

I've seen this movie, I thought, as I watched men play sloppy, inarticulate games of Ping-Pong by the first-floor bar; as I walked onto empty elevators laced with aftershave; as I opened the fridge on the Sales floor to find it full of half-and-half. I've read this book before.

It seemed like half the tech workers I knew were starting to be interested in socialism—or, at least, interested in joking about it on social media, where people shared cat memes (Socialism meow!) and joked about disrupting capitalism. Something was stirring, or taking root. People were coming to politics for the first time through their white-collar labor. They were developing theoretical frameworks on the internet; they were beginning to identify with the Worker. They talked about universal basic income over free cocktails at the company bar.

On social media, there were whispers of dissent among people whose avatars were their fursonas. Site reliability engineers posted nuanced Marxist critiques in the middle of their workdays. A labor reckoning for the tech companies seemed to glimmer on the horizon, slowly taking shape.

With another early employee of the analytics startup, Noah was prototyping an app—*application*—to facilitate collective action in the workplace. "The critique, of course, is that we're monetizing labor organizing," Noah said when I went to see him in Berkeley. His cofounder saw it as a way to make capitalism function better, more efficiently; needless to say, the latter would be the investor pitch. They had considered going through the seed accelerator, until doing thirty seconds of research: *Any industry that still has unions has potential energy that could be released by startups*, the seed accelerator's founder had microblogged. The accelerator claimed to want people who wanted to beat the system, but a tool for organizing workers was perhaps beating the system too hard. The wrong type of collaboration software.

At HQ, I cautiously expressed my excitement about the prospect of a tech workers' union to an engineer. Maybe people would acknowledge the security guards if they had a shared interest, I said. Maybe the money would spread out a little bit. Maybe the people building the tools could have a say in how those tools were used. Maybe we shouldn't all be so quick to identify with charismatic CEOs; maybe we shouldn't assume that the money and the perks and the job market would be there forever; maybe we should factor in the possibility that we might age out. What were we doing, anyway, helping people become billionaires? Billionaires were the mark of a sick society. They shouldn't exist. There was no moral structure in which such a vast accumulation of wealth should be acceptable.

"Please don't start quoting Marx, telling me that our co-workers need to seize the means of production," the engineer said, shaking his head. He had grown up poor, he reminded me; he had spent years working on actual assembly lines before teaching himself to code. "It's not about a means of solidarity or longevity for them. It's just about personal leverage. When I was exposed to asbestos, nobody doing comp-sci at an Ivy League was showing up to help." I had not chosen the right audience. I was not prepared for this argument.

This was just the next phase of the artisanal fetish, the engineer said. It was like LARPing, like Burning Man. "It's a working-class MMOG," he said, shooting me a withering look. "We are not vulnerable people."

I felt ashamed about my own class privilege, everything I took for granted. My closest brush with manual labor was breaking down cardboard boxes in the basement of an independent bookstore. I retrieved additional seltzer waters for us, tangerine flavor. We made uneasy jokes about what a tech workers' union would strike for: ergonomic keyboards, a more inclusive office dog policy. I couldn't elevate the mood. Neither of us could let it go.

"People need unions to feel safe," the engineer said. "What would a union protect any of us from? Uncomfortable conversations?"

Our remote coworkers had wants. They often spoke of feeling like second-class citizens. As the company became more corporate, the culture had gone from remote-first to remote-friendly. The startup's early techno-utopianism did not scale—though not for lack of trying.

In an internal discussion, some of the remote employees campaigned for perks. Food and drink were supplied at the San Francisco headquarters, noted a woman who identified as a digital nomad; a snack and drink allowance for remote employees seemed only fair. *I work from a coffee shop*, she wrote. *I have to buy something when I'm there, and I don't even drink coffee.*

HQ also had a cleaning crew, someone pointed out. *Definitely wouldn't say no to an allowance for a housekeeper*, he added, in case he was being unclear.

A modest yearly budget for home office improvements would be useful, wrote an engineer. He listed items that could not be expensed: office plants; mini-fridges; wall decorations; furniture maintenance.

Flights over four hours long could be booked in business class, posted a salesperson. *I would do a better job representing the company if I could nap on the flight.*

Home gym equipment, someone else said. A road bike, or a good pair of running shoes—a surfboard, or skis. *We could get signed up for one of those snack subscription boxes*, suggested a support representative whose modesty moved me.

I'd like to see more flexibility in the fitness benefit, wrote another engineer. *I'm not comfortable in gyms, so paintball makes up the majority of my physical fitness regimen. It'd be nice to use the benefit to pay for equipment, and paint.*

My engineer comrade sent me a link to the thread. *This is exactly what I'm talking about*, he wrote. *Read this, then tell me you still want to give these people any power.*

A software developer I knew through mutual friends invited himself over to HQ for lunch. He had never been inside the office, he said. He was dying to see it. Working at a company beloved by engineers had given me unearned credibility; I didn't tell him that I almost always worked from home these days, in sagging leggings.

When the developer arrived at the office, something about

him seemed different. A certain swagger. He had always been well-dressed, in a machine-washable way, but he had rolled up wearing a leather jacket and aviator sunglasses. I surveilled him warily as he surveyed the rows of unoccupied standup desks. "So this is where it all happens," he said, nodding approvingly. I had forgotten how much the open-source startup meant to people on the outside. The developer had only ever worked for large corporations, he told me: a cog in the machine. Nothing like this.

We brought lunch up to the roof deck and sat in the sun. Strings of café lights swung above double-wide deck chairs protected by a privacy barrier of palm fronds. In the pool of the apartment complex next door, a woman swam slow and elegant laps. The day inspired lethargy. I wanted to stretch out in one of the padded white lounge chairs with a novel. I wanted someone in a position of authority to remind me to apply sunscreen.

The developer and I ate soba noodles and made small talk. After half an hour or so, he folded his napkin, placed it in the takeout container, and asked, casually, whether I was familiar with a news story about a batch of documents that had been leaked by an anonymous source. It had happened months ago, but it had been in the headlines for days: the documents had exposed personal information about a spate of high-profile politicians, billionaires, and businesspeople. It was an indictment of undemocratic activity perpetrated by the very rich. Newspapers were still publishing stories about the fallout.

Of course, I said. I asked why he mentioned it.

The developer leaned back in his chair and shot me a tilted smirk. In a subtle, swift gesture, he raised his hands and pointed both thumbs at his chest.

•

I was furious. I didn't know what to do with this information; I wondered if it was even true. The developer's reason for telling me, he had explained, was that he was disappointed in the media coverage. He wanted to communicate that abuses of power could be exposed by ordinary citizens—he didn't have an intelligence background, he just cared about structural inequality—and that most conspiracies were mundane. The things that moved history, he said, were often random and serendipitous. He wanted to find someone who would relay his story with more action—more character. He thought I might know journalists in New York who could help.

Journalists in New York told me the story had passed. Still, I couldn't stop thinking about it. I appreciated that there were engineers who still saw the skill set as potentially subversive, in service of the greater good, and not just individually lucrative. All these people, spending their twenties and thirties in open-plan offices on the campuses of the decade's most valuable public companies, pouring themselves bowls of free cereal from human bird feeders, crushing empty cans of fruit-tinged water, bored out of their minds but unable to walk away from the direct deposits—it was so unimaginative. There was so much potential in Silicon Valley, and so much of it just pooled around ad tech, the spillway of the internet economy.

I liked thinking that some of the programmers I passed on the street every day might also be growing disillusioned with the enterprise. That they wanted something better—more. That they intimately understood the global system to which they were contributing, and wanted to change it, and were willing to put themselves on the line. As someone who preferred above-board processes, it scared the shit out of me. It also inspired a feeling like excitement, or hope.

Northern California did not offer a natural human experience of the passage of time. I was confused by the abundance of postcolonial, non-native flora. I was always eating expired yogurts. I was always actively trying to recall the season. I hadn't seen rain in three years. It was no wonder San Francisco was referred to as a city of Peter Pans; no wonder so many people tried to live in the perpetual present. It was easy to forget that anyone was getting older, or that anyone ever would.

"I've been living like someone in her twenties for over a decade," a coworker observed one afternoon, as we idled around the office bar. "I'm almost forty. Why am I going to three concerts a week? Wasn't I supposed to have children?"

A group of our coworkers were already shaking cocktails and pulling drafts. Someone had opened a bottle of pink prosecco. Two men in matching hoodies played a loose game of shuffleboard, and engineers at the Ping-Pong table dutifully ticked the ball back and forth. Through the floor-to-ceiling windows behind the DJ booth, I watched a man lying on the sidewalk, pants pulled down to midthigh, napping on his side in the sun.

"My friends back home are fighting with their spouses about mortgages," my coworker said. She looked into the murk of her coffee cup and sighed. "What does this all look like when everyone gets older? When does this stop being fun?"

Was it still fun? Was it ever? I had turned twenty-nine that summer, and I was starting to want things I had not wanted when I was twenty-five. I developed the bad habit of swiping through real estate apps thirstily, like I was waiting for a gut-renovated Victorian in Cole Valley to ask me, unsolicited, for my Myers-Briggs type.

I began pointing to babies in the street as if I had only ever seen one in an encyclopedia. Look, I would say to Ian—a baby! Like we were bird-watching. Like I had just seen a shooting star.

To celebrate his birthday, Patrick threw a small party at a campsite, technically a horse camp, near Muir Woods. *Someone has kindly volunteered to help hold up the equine side of the bargain*, the invitation read. *Arriving in the saddle is warmly encouraged*.

The following weekend, Ian and I arrived at the horse camp to find a group of computer scientists in outdoor apparel assembling, somewhat inefficiently, a trough of salad. Several slabs of salmon lay on the grill. The corrals were empty. "Ah, you know San Francisco," said a cheerful entrepreneur in a fleece vest, when I inquired after the equine side of the bargain. "Even the horses are flaky."

Ian fell into conversation with an engineer he admired, a designer of conceptual, experimental user interfaces. It was rare for me to hear him talk about computer science. He was so reticent when it came to his job that I easily forgot how much he loved the work, the puzzles, the magic of it. I sat on a picnic table and tried to insinuate myself into a conversation between two engineers discussing young adult literature.

I had not spent a ton of time with Patrick around other people, but I had spent enough to know I was an outlier in his social circle, which was largely composed of scientists, entrepreneurs, and technologists. I often felt embarrassed to tell this crowd that I worked in customer support, then felt angry about my embarrassment. It did not help that whenever I felt insecure, I tended to get combative, or pushy, or in over my head. I was always roping founders into debates about whether or not crowdsourced reviewing sites constituted "a literature." I was always making unprompted arguments against privatization, picking fights.

The mood was upbeat and polite. I managed to behave myself. Conversation rose and died down. When Patrick spoke, people outside of his immediate radius fell quiet and listened, like he was an oracle. Then again, I wanted to listen, too.

The salmon came off the grill and we incorporated it into the salad, gathering around the picnic tables to eat. Halfway through dinner, another skinny man in outdoor apparel bounded onto the campsite, carrying a plastic bag. Patrick leaped up in excitement. Inside the bag, he explained, were two continuous glucose monitors with digital readers. The monitors were difficult to procure in the United States, and the readers had to be imported. We all watched as he unwrapped the package and punched a sensor into his own shoulder, wincing. I tried to exchange a meaningful look with Ian. Patrick did not have diabetes. "What?" Ian said. "Seems cool. I'd try one."

After a while, someone brought out a small cake and a candle. We sang "Happy Birthday" while Patrick turned pink.

"Well then," he said, when the singing was over and conversation did not resume. "Shall we put out the fire?" I suggested we leave it burning. We could set up our tents, then drink whiskey and talk until it got too late or too cold. This was always my favorite part of camping: everyone swapping intimacies and confidences, leaning into the evening as time slowed. I was excited for it, eager to find common ground, see everyone relax a little bit. Patrick seemed confused.

I looked around the group. It became very clear, very quickly, that the plan had never been to camp out. Ian and I were alone in having brought a tent. Within ten minutes, the party had been disassembled and packed into paper bags, the grills scraped, the recycling sorted. People filtered out into the night in carpool configurations, carrying leftovers and coolers. Flashlight beams floated out into the road and disappeared around a curve. It wasn't yet ten o'clock.

"I guess we have the place to ourselves," Ian said, looking around. It suddenly seemed ridiculous that we should be camping out by ourselves in the middle of an outdoor stable in Marin. The site felt exposed, comically large. The corrals glinted. I wondered if park rangers might come through, and if so, whether we would be on the hook for a horse. Would we be fined? It was state land. Were we breaking a law? Why had I thought we were all going to sleep there, like people with nothing to do the next day? Part of me felt bad that they had other things to take care of that weekend, when my only plan was to build a fruit-fly trap. Part of me felt indignant. I didn't want to feel ashamed about being unproductive, for wanting to drink whiskey and make up fake constellations.

We should just go back, I said. Ian shook his head—he'd had a couple of beers, and I didn't know how to drive stick. The roads were unlit and winding. We set up the tent and brushed our teeth, stamping out our spit in the dirt, then lay in parallel sleeping bags, listening to the redwoods bend in the wind.

Though I did not want what Patrick and his friends wanted, there was still something appealing to me about the lives they had chosen. I envied their focus, their commitment, their ability to know what they wanted, and to say it out loud—the same things I always envied. They were all so accomplished, and athletic. It didn't help that I hardly understood what most of them did, I just knew they were good at it.

At twenty-eight, Patrick had built something sophisticated and sprawling, something useful that people seemed to love. I wondered what would happen if he and his friends went on to run the industry, as it seemed they might. I also wondered what it might mean on a personal level. Our friendship already demanded a certain amount of compartmentalization, presumably from both sides. I wondered if money and status would change him; I wondered whether I would become a liability. I worried that people in his position often had no choice but to conform to certain expectations: the system they were accountable to wasn't just powerful, it was a machine. Patrick was idealistic and independent, but it seemed that the professional demands and social mores of his structural position could eventually require that he work against himself. It was strange to see him form a public identity on social media—strange that he had followers, a fan base—and from time to time, he would endorse publications or policies or positions that surprised me. I had a hard time with this. The private person was funny, thoughtful, open-minded. But the public persona, with whom I often disagreed, had growing amplification, influence, and power.

I shared some of this with Ian, who was reading by headlamp. He shrugged, the light bobbing across the fly. "I think you're underestimating what you might have that they don't," he said.

You? I asked, turning on my side to face him. "That's sweet," he said. "But bigger than that, I think. Just something worth considering."

It seemed to me that whatever I had, that the men of Silicon Valley did not, was exactly what I had been trying to sublimate for the past four years. Working in tech had provided an escape from the side of my personality that was emotional, impractical, ambivalent, and inconvenient—the part of me that wanted to know everyone's feelings, that wanted to be moved, that had no apparent market value.

Eventually, I would acknowledge that these qualities weren't actually less valuable, in noneconomic terms, than what the founders and technologists prioritized. They weren't more valuable, either; just different. My reasons for deflecting and deferring were pragmatic—money, social affirmation, a sense of stability—but they were also personal. I still clung to the belief that I could find meaning and fulfillment in work—the result of over two decades of educational affirmation, parental encouragement, socioeconomic privilege, and generational mythology. Unlike the men, I didn't know how to articulate what I wanted. Safer, then, to join a group that told itself, and the world, that it was superior: a hedge against uncertainty, isolation, insecurity.

These motivations were not aging well. In reality, there was nothing superior about those whom I was trying to impress. Most were smart and nice and ambitious, but so were a lot of people. The novelty was burning off; the industry's pervasive idealism was increasingly dubious. Tech, for the most part, wasn't progress. It was just business.

This was both a relief and a disappointment. It was also, perhaps, the root of my empathy for the young entrepreneurs of Silicon Valley. Many of them were at least a decade deep into lives they had selected for themselves as teenagers. Surely, I thought, some must have wanted to try something different, get off the ride. Surely some were beginning to have moral, spiritual, political misgivings. I was radiant with projections.

I did think about what the endgame could look like. I saw myself pursuing success as a nontechnical woman in tech: becoming a middle manager, then an executive, then a consultant or coach who spoke at conferences, to inspire more women. I could see myself onstage, forcing a smile and holding a clicker, feeling my curls go limp in real time. I could see myself writing blog posts on my own personal business philosophy: *How to Squander Opportunity. How Not to Negotiate. How to Cry in Front of Your Boss.* I would work twice as hard as my male counterparts to be taken half as seriously. I would devote my time and energy to a corporation, and hope that it was reciprocal. I would make decisions based on the market that were rewarded by the market, and feel important, because I would feel right.

I liked feeling right; I loved feeling right. Unfortunately, I also wanted to feel good. I wanted to find a way, while I could, to engage with my own life.

For a long time, I harbored the belief that there was a yearning at the heart of entrepreneurial ambition, a tender dimension that no one wanted to acknowledge. Some spiritual aspect beneath the in-office yoga classes and meditation apps and selective Stoicism and circular thought-leading. How else to explain the rituals and congregations, the conferences and off-sites, the corporate revival meetings, startup fealty and fanaticism—the gospel of work, modernized and optimized? I was committed to the idea of vulnerability.

All these boys, wandering around, nimble and paranoid and prone to extremes, pushing against the world until they found the parts that would bend to them. I assumed they had people to impress, parents to please, siblings to rival, rivals to beat. I assumed their true desires were relatable: community, or intimacy, to simply be loved and understood. I knew that building systems, and getting them to work, was its own deep satisfaction—but I assumed everyone wanted more.

I was always looking for the emotional narrative, the psychological explanation, the personal history. Some exculpatory story on which to train my sympathy. It wasn't so simple as wanting to believe that adulthood was a psychic untangling of adolescence, willful revisionist history. My obsession with the spiritual, sentimental, and political possibilities of the entrepreneurial class was an ineffectual attempt to alleviate my own guilt about participating in a globally extractive project, but more important, it was a projection: they would become the next power elite. I wanted to believe that as generations turned over, those coming into economic and political power would build a different, better, more expansive world, and not just for people like themselves.

Later, I would mourn these conceits. Not only because this version of the future was constitutionally impossible—such arbitrary and unaccountable power was, after all, the problem—but also because I was repeating myself. I was looking for stories; I should have seen a system.

The young men of Silicon Valley were doing fine. They loved their industry, loved their work, loved solving problems. They had no qualms. They were builders by nature, or so they believed. They saw markets in everything, and only opportunities. They had inexorable faith in their own ideas and their own potential. They were ecstatic about the future. They had power, wealth, and control. The person with the yearning was me.

We were too old to use innocence as an excuse. Hubris, maybe. Indifference, preoccupation. Idealism. A certain complacency endemic to people for whom things had, in recent years, turned out okay. We had assumed it would all blow over. We had just been so busy with work, lately.

When it started to look like perhaps we were wrong—perhaps the United States presidency might actually go to a real estate developer who had once played the part of a successful businessman on reality television—everyone came up with a last-ditch, Hail Mary pass at civic participation. A group of founders poured money into get-out-the-vote initiatives, trying to encourage millennials to perform an in-person task via targeted advertising on mobile apps and social networks. Digital donations flowed. The open-source startup decided it would run a banner on Election Day, reminding users in the United States that it was Election Day.

In the grand tradition of affluent white Americans living in coastal cities in times of political crisis and social upheaval, I had turned inward. I thought we had it in the bag. I saw Silicon

Valley as an unstoppable train; I had bought into tech's self-flattering grandiosity, and trusted things would turn around in its favor. I didn't know who was more delusional: the entrepreneurial class, for thinking they could change the trajectory of history—or me, for believing them.

At the beginning of November, I opened my laptop to find the Terms of Service team puzzling over a repository that claimed to be compiling research on a sex-trafficking and pedophilia ring run out of a pizzeria in Washington, D.C. I scrolled through chat backlog, trying to catch up. The content had something to do with leaked emails from the presidential campaign, but everything was blurring together. It all carried a whiff of conspiratorial thinking.

I couldn't bring myself to engage. I didn't know what I was looking at, and didn't want to. My teammates seemed to have it under control. I felt a deep gratitude for them, their willingness to tackle flare-ups; their good humor and curiosity about the matted underbelly of the internet. I turned my attention to copyright takedowns as they dropped emojis of spinning slices of pizza into our team chat. I didn't give the repository a second thought, until it was all over the news.

Later, I would wonder if I had missed it because I was more of a product of the tech industry—with its context aversion, and emphasis on speed and scale, its overwhelming myopia—than I wanted to admit. Or maybe it was personal; maybe I wasn't analytical. Maybe I wasn't a systems thinker.

Even so: the systems thinkers missed it, too.

Patrick and I met for dinner. I found him sitting in the back of the restaurant, reading the house zine. He waited for me to shrug off my coat, then leaned across the table. "Is winter coming for the tech industry?" he asked. It was never winter in San Francisco, I thought; it was always winter. Mark Twain. Then I realized he was referencing a popular fantasy novel: winter meant the other shoe dropping.

There had been increased attention on Silicon Valley during the campaign season. The same publications that had, until recently, analyzed tech companies' cafeteria selections with a level of detail usually reserved for SEC filings were beginning to reconsider the booster position. People were beginning to talk about antitrust, consumer product safety regulations, patent and copyright law. They were beginning to turn a critical eye to internet addiction and the ways tech companies were exacerbating economic inequality. They were catching on to the misinformation and conspiratorial content spreading across social networks. The industry was used to getting attention, but not like this.

The tech industry would be fine, I said, dipping a piece of bread into a trough of olive oil. If a reckoning was coming for tech, and a result was fewer startups making collaboration software or selling button-down shirts or underpaying contract workers, that didn't seem like the end of the world to me. I was not worried about the tech industry. In any case, there seemed to be much graver possibilities. Patrick nodded. He looked as exhausted as I felt. It wasn't the moment to relitigate the virtues of the Valley.

I wanted the optimistic perspective on what might happen, I said. What did he have for me? I was so used to him pushing a counternarrative, cheering me up, making the future feel new. He was so productive, so effective. Surely he had ideas about solutions. Patrick looked down at his hands. "I really don't know," he said. "It's quite dire."

Toward the end of our meal, he apologized—he had to take a work call, he said, but it wouldn't be long. His company was in the final stage of closing a new round. Just an extra anchor in the future. There was so much political uncertainty. We split the check and left, zipping our black down jackets against the cold.

Patrick joined a conference call as we walked down Folsom Street. The streets were dark, abandoned. He took a tablet out of his backpack, opened his email, and used a finger to scribble his signature on several documents. I was struck by the comfort and confidence with which he moved, very literally, through the world. I tried to loosen my grip on the handles of my tote bag.

We passed beneath the elevated highway, toward SoMa. I glanced at Patrick, who was chatting happily in brisk, complete paragraphs. If winter *did* come, I wondered what that would mean for him. I had no concept of the stakes. I couldn't decide which one of us thought we had more to lose.

A few weeks later, reading the heavily moderated message board, I would come to an easy conclusion. The commentariat was discussing Patrick's startup, which had been in the news for its latest fund-raising round: the valuation was among the Valley's highest for private companies. In the ambient light beneath the freeway that night, he had become one of the youngest self-made billionaires.

I called the developer who had claimed he was responsible for the high-profile leak. Is there anything you can do? I asked, feeling like a child. I pawed at the carpet with my foot.

He was quiet for a moment. "I'm not exactly sure what you're asking for," he said. "This is really slow work. It could take months, and there's no guarantee." I wasn't exactly sure what I was after either. Some validation of the utopian belief in information. Some justification of the networks, humming along at scale. Anyway, there weren't months. There were just a few days.

I drove up to Reno with two friends from college and a coworker from the Sales team. We checked into an undersea-themed casino, like a bachelorette party with nothing to celebrate. None of us had thought to bring a swimsuit for the casino's pools; none of us played the slots. We wandered the grounds and channeled our discomfort into social media consumables, posting photos of the casino's indoor palm trees and illuminated water features, fountains of spurting mermen and dolphins backlit blue. We lay two to a bed in our room that night, sleepless and alert in the dark.

The next morning, we made our way to a volunteer center, turning in to a strip mall behind an electric car with California plates. As we stood in line for clipboards, I realized I did not know where we were. We had plugged the address into a mapping app and followed it blindly, just as we had driven up from San Francisco. I could have been anywhere.

The next two days were spent canvassing, walking through suburban sprawl. I hated our conspicuousness, the imposition on strangers; hated that they all knew what was coming the minute we clomped up onto the porch. In working-class neighborhoods with streets that were quiet and still, half the parked cars bore windshield decals from ride-sharing startups. My coworker fretted about rumors she was hearing of the Sales team starting layoffs. PRAY FOR JESUS TO LOWER INFLATION, advised a bumper sticker.

On Election Day, engorged with anxiety and optimism, I

secured an enamel pin shaped like a uterus to my jacket and went to scout breakfast. A line of men sat at the slot machines, smoking. As the woman behind the casino coffee bar rang me up, I asked whether she had a plan in place to vote that day, reciting the opening of a script I still needed to memorize. "Not this year," she said, shaking her head. I was taken aback. I don't blame you, I said, not sure if I meant it.

Few people answered the doorbell that day. We trudged along, sitting on curbs to share water and snacks. One of my college friends wore a nameplate necklace that said NASTY WOMAN and a T-shirt with a cat that read THIS PUSSY GRABS BACK. On my phone, celebrities looked glamorous in thrifted pantsuits, and strangers rubbed linty I VOTED stickers on the graves of suffragettes. A venture capitalist posted a photo of a bottle of champagne beside a bottle of vodka, adding a grayscale filter for historical effect. Friends shared selfies from outside their polling places, faces staunch and optimistic, drenched in fall light. The company chat rooms were uncharacteristically subdued.

Life in the attention economy had made me oblivious. My social media feeds overflowed with feminist slogans, iconography, and products: ceramic vases shaped like naked breasts, baby onesies that read THE FUTURE IS FEMALE. This had been my internet for months.

It did not transfer to suburban Nevada. Women stood behind screen doors and looked at us, with our clipboards and patriotic stickers and aestheticized coastal corporate feminism, and simply shook their heads. At the curve of a cul-de-sac, in an affluent neighborhood of compact SUVs and ornate landscaping, we leaned against our rental car, bent over our phones. I unpinned the uterus and put it in my pocket. It had all seemed possible. It had seemed real. As if in slow motion, I felt the force of the swerve.

The polls were closing. The air was beginning to cool.

EPILOGUE

For months after the election, my friends and coworkers were not doing well. Stomachaches, insomnia, astrology. They drank too much. They took up moderate vaping. They went to meditative sound baths and considered microdosing to stave off looming depression or regain lost productivity. They appended their email salutations with phrases like "given the circumstances" and "despite the news." Everyone engaged in deep and irresponsible magical thinking.

On the heavily moderated message board, the commentariat discussed a Marshall Plan of rationality, a new enlightenment. On social media, a sales leader at an education software company suggested crowdfunding private planes to fly over red counties and drop leaflets with facts about the travel ban, and a former executive at the analytics startup asked his connections if anyone could recommend a place to buy gold bars. *Time to get good at crypto*, everyone said. Those of us in or adjacent to the tech industry advised friends and family members to download encrypted communications apps. Our solution, as ever: more technology.

CEOs and venture capitalists, oh-shit patriots with fiduciary duties, extended olive branches to elected officials. Industry leaders protested in the airports, or at least posed for photographs. They advocated for more generous immigration policies, prioritizing immigrants who knew how to code.

Everyone was staying up late, anxiety-scrolling, and the advertising algorithms stayed up, too. Friends bought weighted blankets designed for people with sensory processing disorders, marketed to them on social media, and lay underneath with their arms at their sides, waiting for the oxytocin to drop. Fascist ideology and paranoid conspiracies circulated. Hoaxing and misinformation and memes, long the trappings of message-board culture, moved into the civic sphere. Trolling was a new political currency.

There was Nazi iconography in the news, and Nazi rhetoric in the Terms of Service team inbox. Our field was still new, and not unified. Depending on the company, our work was called Policy, or Community Policy, or Trust and Safety, or Community and Safety, or, simply, Safety; depending on the company, the team was six years or six months old. No one was equipped to adjudicate speech for the millions of people spending their lives online. Outside the industry, people argued about the First Amendment. Inside, we were calculating risk, determining the seriousness of threats, trying to react thoughtfully but nimbly. The nature of online abuse evolved quickly; it was always just a little out of grasp.

At a gathering of people in the field, a high-level employee of a household-name startup approached me to talk about our industry's new burden of responsibility. We balanced paper plates covered in cheese and fruit. We passed our anxieties back and forth. My interlocutor leaned in conspiratorially. "There are no adults in the White House," he said, with a trace of a smile. "We're the government now."

•

I thought, for a while, that everything would change. I thought that the party was over. I thought the industry was in for a reckoning, that it was the beginning of the end, that what I had experienced in San Francisco was the final stage of a prelapsarian era, the end of our generational Gold Rush, an unsustainable age of excess.

Then I left the house. There was the world, with its addicts and joggers, its fortified strollers and leather boutiques and swishing eucalyptus, everything bright and intact. Cranes swung over warehouses stuffed with new transplants. Shuttles crested the hills, riding the brakes on descent. The city and the industry, bound by the ecosystem, continued to cycle and churn.

I could have stayed in my job forever, which was how I knew it was time to go. The money and the ease of the lifestyle weren't enough to mitigate the emotional drag of the work: the burnout, the repetition, the intermittent toxicity. The days did not feel distinct. I felt a widening emptiness, rattling around my studio every morning, rotating in my desk chair. I had the luxury, if not the courage, to do something about it.

In early 2018, I left the open-source startup. I wanted a change, and I wanted to write. My impulse, over the past few years, had been to remove myself from my own life, to watch from the periphery and try to see the vectors, the scaffolding, the systems at play. Psychologists might refer to this as dissociation; I considered it the sociological approach. It was, for me, a way out of unhappiness. It did make things more interesting.

Leaving a remote workplace was anticlimactic. On my last day, I had a sixty-second exit interview, conducted over video chat. I dropped a waving-hand emoji into the Terms of Service chat room and posted a brief farewell to the company's internal message board. *I didn't know you worked here*, wrote a colleague, in the comments. Then I sat on my bed with my laptop, watching my access to internal platforms be revoked, one by one. Every 404 error like a light going out. A whole world, zippered up—easy come, easy go.

After three and a half years, most of my employee options had vested. I was ambivalent about exercising them, despite the rumors of a pending acquisition: the stock was not cheap, and I was uncertain that it would amount to anything.

I convinced myself I had to play the game. On the ninetieth day of my ninety-day purchase window, I hand-delivered a check to HQ for the entirety of my savings account, to buy as many of my vested options as I could. As I stood in the guest entrance, waiting for the stock plan administrator to collect the paperwork, I watched my former coworkers chatting happily with one another in the on-site coffee shop and felt, wrenchingly, that leaving had been a huge mistake.

Certain unflattering truths: I had felt unassailable behind the walls of power. Society was shifting, and I felt safer inside the empire, inside the machine. It was preferable to be on the side that did the watching than on the side being watched.

Former employees of the open-source startup still hung out in a chat room, an unaffiliated alumni club where people tried to poach one another for their startups between debates over whether or not our stock options would ever be worth anything. They talked shit and traded speculative financial advice. They continued to swap photographs of their home-office setups and their octopus-cat stuffed animals. They waxed nostalgic about early employee summits, lost weekends, blowout parties in the office. That time they completed a team-building treasure hunt involving selfies with a stripper. That time they stashed acid at HQ. Their reminiscences hardened into shared mythology. Stories I knew, a shadow oral history, remained untold.

In June, news broke that the open-source startup had been purchased for seven and a half billion dollars, by the highly litigious Seattle-based conglomerate. The conglomerate had, in the nineties, attempted to stomp down the open-source software movement—but this was a new era, insisted everyone involved in the deal.

In the ex-employee chat room, people compared second-hand information about the share price; they posted celebratory photographs of themselves in octopus-cat T-shirts. *TFW you wake up retired,* wrote one of the early employees. Another expressed her ambivalence about the windfall. *It's like having a conflict diamond,* she wrote. *It's valuable, but it came at an unforgivable human cost.*

Not just a diamond, a mine. A significant fraction of my former coworkers became millionaires and multimillionaires; the founders became billionaires. The venture capitalists refueled. I was happy for friends, especially lower-level employees who had worked incredibly hard, and I was excited for their families, for whom a low-six-figure exit would be life-changing. I wondered if the company would develop an internal class hierarchy, then remembered it already had one.

The shares I exercised were worth about two hundred thousand dollars, before taxes. This was a windfall by my standards, if modest for the industry: it was less than the median salary at the social network everyone hated; less than the six hundred thousand dollars direct-deposited into an early support rep's bank account; less than the multimillion-dollar sums that went to people I suspected had done indelible harm to coworkers. I felt no pride, only relief and guilt.

I was lucky. Draining my bank account to exercise my stock options was only tenable because I knew I could borrow money from family, or from Ian. Some of my coworkers, largely women in nontechnical roles whose work had been foundational to the company, but whose salaries did not allow them to save much in the city with the highest cost of living in the country, had been offered generous stock grants that they were unable to exercise after they left the company. Some women, I had heard, were promised extensions on their exercise windows, only to have the extensions vetoed by the board after the grants had expired. The acquisition was a once-in-a-lifetime bonanza. It passed them by.

Flat structure, meritocracy, non-nonnegotiable offers. Systems do work as designed.

That same spring, the CEO of the analytics startup stepped down. "I just need a break," he told a business reporter. "It's been a marathon." On social media, he joined the ranks of industry thought-leaders contributing to the founder-realism genre, recommending therapy and community, microblogging his own emotional development in real time.

In the chat room for ex-employees of the analytics startup, my former coworkers lauded the decision. They joked about inviting the CEO to the channel. They rolled their emoji-eyes at his inspirational posts. They reminisced about the early team, griped about the CEO, and debated, as former employees of still-private companies were wont to do, whether our own stock options would ever be worth anything. I wondered if it had been traumatic for the CEO to leave the company he built, if it felt like grief. I wondered if he had regrets, and how long it would be until he did it all again.

Within a year of the CEO's departure, the CTO and several engineers would return to the analytics startup to see it through. I wondered if they felt a loyalty to the product—if they would not be satisfied until the problem, technically speaking, was solved. I understood the appeal of returning to the company, though I knew I never could. It wasn't just that I had traded the security of tech for more engaging work—and was hoping, against the odds, that it would last—but that I couldn't imagine once again being so complaisant, so consumed.

A few months later, I wandered through the Mission, killing time before meeting a friend for lunch. Sitting outside a fast-casual Greek restaurant on Valencia Street were two men engaged in animated conversation, their napkins wadded on the table. Nearly five years had passed, but I recognized the CEO of the analytics startup immediately: gelled hair, slight frame, green jacket. He looked happy, relaxed, older. He looked just like anyone else.

Weekday lunch on the town, I thought—good for him. Then I turned and walked as quickly as possible in the opposite direction. I am confident he never saw me.

ACKNOWLEDGMENTS

I am immensely grateful to Daniel Levin Becker, Molly Fischer, Henry Freedland, Jen Gann, Sam MacLaughlin, Manjula Martin, Emily Nakashima, Meaghan O'Connell, Hannah Schneider, and Taylor Sperry, for their intellectual generosity and editorial insight. I am thankful to Nick Friedman for early, foundational conversations. Thank you to Moira Weigel for her friendship and intelligence, and for always offering the systems view. Thank you to Gideon Lewis-Kraus, for wild kindness at every stage.

Thank you to Mark Krotov, for genius edits and unfailing support of this project. Thank you to Dayna Tortorici, for encouraging me to write about San Francisco and startup culture in 2015, and for brilliant editorial advice. I am indebted to *n+1*: thank you for taking a chance on me.

Thank you to Chris Parris-Lamb, for developing this book alongside me, and for being a constant source of wisdom, advice, clarity, humor, and support; truly beyond. Thank you to Sarah Bolling, for sharp and understanding notes, and to Rebecca Gardner, Ellen Goodson Coughtrey, and Will Roberts, for bringing this book to readers abroad.

Thank you to my editor, Emily Bell, for believing in this project from the beginning, and for being a fierce advocate at every stage. Thank you to the team at MCD / Farrar, Straus and Giroux, especially Jackson Howard, Naomi Huffman, Sean McDonald, and Sarita Varma. Thank you to Rebecca Caine for her thoughtfulness and poise while working on this manuscript, and to Greg Villepique, Chandra Wohleber, Kylie Byrd, Kathleen Cook, Nina Frieman, Jonathan Lippincott, and Gretchen Achilles, for their attention and care. Thank you to Anna Kelly, Caspian Dennis, and Sarah Thickett, for championing this book in the U.K.

Thank you to Jason Richman, for his exuberance and insight, and to his team at UTA. Thank you to Johnny Pariseau and Alison Small, for their excitement, integrity, and open-mindedness. Thank you to Michael De Luca Productions and Brownstone Productions. I am grateful to Sara'o Bery for his frank, crucial advice.

Thank you to Emily Stokes, for working closely on sections of this book, and for being a wise and generous sounding board. Thank you to Michael Luo, Pamela McCarthy, David Remnick, and Dorothy Wickenden for offering me a place to continue writing about tech culture. Thank you to Carla Blumenkranz, Anthony Lydgate, and Daniel Zalewski. Thank you to Joshua Rothman for his insightful, enriching editing on my Silicon Valley dispatches.

Thank you to Leah Campbell, Danilo Campos, Patrick Collison, Parker Higgins, Cameron Spickert, and Kyle Warren, for their friendship and trust. Thank you to David Gumbiner. Thank you to my former coworkers at the analytics and open-source startups, especially those who took the time, and some risk, to speak with me for this project. Thank you to dear friends in California and New York, so many of whom have helped untangle my thoughts about labor, life, art, capitalism—like anything, a work in progress.

Thank you to the Shermans, north and south, for their kindness and encouragement. Thank you to my family, especially David and Marina Wiener. Thank you to Dan Wiener and Ellen Freudenheim, for their enthusiasm and guidance. I am grateful to Ian Sherman for his love, for his steady support of my writing, and for always asking the right questions.